Tiger Moon

Tiger Moon

Fiona Sunquist
Mel Sunquist

The University of Chicago Press
Chicago and London

Fiona Sunquist was born in Bombay, India, and is a wildlife writer and frequent contributor to *International Wildlife*. Mel Sunquist is a wildlife ecologist at the University of Florida. He has done field work on snow leopards, bobcats, leopards, and wild dogs, and together the Sunquists have studied ocelots in Venezuela.

The University of Chicago Press, Chicago 60637
The University of Chicago Press, Ltd., London
© 1988 by The University of Chicago
All rights reserved. Published 1988
Printed in the United States of America

97 96 95 94 93 92 91 90 89 88   5 4 3 2 1

Library of Congress Cataloging in Publication Data

Sunquist, Fiona.
  Tiger moon.

  Bibliography: p.
  Includes index.
  1. Tigers—Nepal—Royal Chitwan National Park.
2. Wildlife conservation—Nepal—Royal Chitwan
National Park.   3. Natural history—Nepal—Royal
Chitwan National Park.   4. Royal Chitwan National
Park (Nepal)   I. Sunquist, Melvin E.   II. Title.
QL737.C23S86   1988   639.9'7974428   87-25504
ISBN 0-226-78001-5

For Rita and Campbell

Contents

Prologue

"This can't be the same stuff that grows on lawns," I thought as I followed Mel through an undulating mass of greenery. It was a forest of grass, tall as trees. "There are rhinos in here," Mel said casually, parting the grass carefully in front of him. "This is not the best section of trail, but it gets easier later on."

It was my first look at the tiger study site in Royal Chitwan National Park, the place that was to be our home for the next two years. Mel had arrived in Nepal a few months earlier to begin work on the Smithsonian Tiger Ecology Project, and I had just joined him. We would walk this trail daily as part of the routine search for radio-collared tigers. "When you said grassland, I was thinking more of the African Seregenti," I murmured mutinously. "You can't see your hand in front of your face in this."

The grass ended abruptly in a ten-foot sandy bank topped with trees. The path followed the edge of the forest, winding among the trees, and walking became easier. We could see into the tall grass now, where a flurry of small birds pecked and hopped among the stems. Beyond the grass was a river, and distant hills marked the boundary between Nepal and India. Pairs of gold-colored ducks spiraled down to land on the water, and an elephant with a man on its back moved slowly along the opposite bank.

I began to feel more optimistic and started to say so, but Mel brusquely motioned me to silence. He grabbed my arm. "Quick, follow me," he said urgently, then sprinted off down the trail through the forest. I stood there for a few seconds while his words sank in, then rushed after him, shouting "Wait!" By the time I caught up he was six feet up a tree, his hand stretched down toward me. "Up here, quickly," he whispered, and as I started to say "I can't," he hauled me off the ground and shoved me roughly onto a branch above him.

Bewildered and not a little angry, I turned to speak, then followed Mel's silent gaze to the large gray outline of a rhino. It was standing on the path next to the place where we had emerged from the grass. The rhino jerked its head from side to side, sniffed the air, then charged. Bursting through tangled vegetation, it ignored the path and rushed straight at our tree. For a moment I thought it was going to hit us, but it swept by, inches below the branch Mel's feet were resting on. As the rhino trotted off through the undergrowth, puffing and snorting, we saw a small pink calf bouncing along in her wake.

For the rest of the afternoon I scuttled nervously from one climbable tree to another, seeing rhinos behind every bush and branch. By the time we reached the river crossing opposite camp, I was almost in tears. Although I have a degree in zoology, I had no experience with large, dangerous animals. All my thoughts of field studies in exotic locations involved sitting in a Land Rover watching lions through binoculars as I had seen biologists do in television documentaries. Mel, who had done fieldwork in Panama and Pakistan, had a much better idea of what we were getting into. It had sounded romantic and adventurous to be going off to study tigers in Nepal, but the reality now seemed much more frightening; a stupid mistake or a moment's inattentiveness could endanger my life. I would have to learn a whole new set of rules to survive.

Before wading through the waist-deep water of the broad Rapti River to reach camp, we sat on the bank and watched the sun go down. From our subtropical world of grassland, jungle, and banana trees, we saw the skyline ablaze with the impossible spectacle of the Himalayas at sunset. The mountains were lit as if from within by the changing pinks and golds of the evening light. As faint, ghostly plumes of snow were swirled from their summits by the high-altitude winds, they seemed like a figment of the imagination, an illusion, a beautiful backdrop painted on a clear, blue bowl of sky.

During the next few days I went through a lot of self-examination. Mel had already settled in and was clearly in love with the place. He talked excitedly about the awe he felt when he had captured and radio collared his first tiger two months earlier, the visceral thrill of seeing the great golden cat wake up and walk off into the forest, and the utter tranquility of the river at dawn when the morning fog curled from the water.

I had two choices. I could either learn the survival skills necessary to work beside Mel in the field or stay in camp and leave the daily trips into the jungle to others. In the end there was no real contest.

View from the river crossing near Sauraha, looking south into the park toward the Siwalik Hills and India.

Curiosity and sheer enchantment overcame my initial terror, and I decided I might never forgive myself if I wasted my opportunity through cowardice. However, my fear of rhinos, acquired on that first outing, remained with me for the rest of the study—rather than diminishing with experience, it grew.

Although this book is written in my words, Mel and I have collaborated on every aspect of the story. Most of the book grew from diaries I kept during our stay in Nepal. We have tried to convey a realistic sense of what it was like to live and work in Nepal, not only the adventure and excitement but also our day-to-day routine. Discomfort, boredom, and mistakes are usually left out of such stories, but we have included them here. Any mistakes were ours alone; no one else was to blame. But we hope people will realize that biologists are not as omniscient as books and films often make them out to be.

Ours was not a field study conducted in a park isolated from people. We lived near a small village, and the project involved a large staff of Nepalis. The people we lived with played a major role in the study and in our lives, and they have an important part in this book.

This is as it should be, because the lives of tigers and man are inextricably intertwined. International councils and wildlife organizations can pass laws and create reserves, but to have any hope of preventing the tigers' extinction, we must also strive to understand the lives of the people who make their homes alongside them.

1   The Mountains Had Wings

*J*N 1974, MEL RECEIVED a call from Ross Simons of the Office of the Assistant Secretary for Science at the Smithsonian Institution. Ross wanted to know if Mel was interested in radio tracking tigers in Nepal. Mel's first reaction was a firm no. He had only just returned from three months of searching for snow leopards in the mountains of northwest Pakistan with George Schaller. All he had seen of the elusive cat was a single set of fresh tracks in the snow. He had contracted an alarming array of intestinal parasites and lost nearly fifty pounds from an already slender frame. At that moment, the last thing he wanted to do was to commit himself to another field study. He had had enough of secretive, nocturnal cats and mountainous terrain.

However, as he recovered his health and did a little research on Nepal, the project began to sound more interesting. The study site was only five hundred feet above sea level and had a dense, undisturbed population of tigers. At least there might be enough animals to make a study feasible. When Ross called back a month later, Mel agreed to go. He left for Nepal in October of 1974, and I joined him six months later.

A hundred years ago there were eight races or subspecies of tigers. Their distribution spanned Asia from Iran and Turkey in the west to China and Korea in the east. Tigers lived in the tropical rainforest of Sumatra and Java on the equator, and among the conifers and hardwoods of Manchuria and Korea in the far north. Today, of the original eight races of tiger, only five survive in the wild. The Javan, Caspian, and Balinese tigers are extinct, while the Chinese, Sumatran, and Siberian races each number less than a few hundred animals. Only the Bengal and Indochinese races are estimated at more than two thousand individuals each.

Although tigers were listed as an endangered species in 1969, they were still being hunted for sport into the early 1970s. The Indian government took the first conservation initiative by banning hunting and enacting legislation to protect the tiger. As it became more obvious that the tiger was in trouble throughout its geographical range, governments of other countries gradually followed suit. However, the development of an effective conservation program was slowed by the lack of accurate information on the tiger's ecology. Even basic data, such as how many tigers there were, did not exist.

The best estimate, or certainly the most often-quoted figure, was that there were forty thousand tigers in India at the turn of the century. E. P. Gee, writing in the early 1960s, estimated the tiger population then at about four thousand. Shortly after the tiger was declared an endangered species, the Indian Department of Forests carried out an extensive census and came up with some frightening statistics. The total tiger population in India was estimated at less than two thousand, with maybe five hundred other tigers scattered throughout Bangladesh, Bhutan, Burma, Nepal, and Sikkim.

Following this alarming news, World Wildlife Fund International launched a "Save the Tiger" campaign and announced "Project Tiger," a multi-million-dollar effort to save the tiger in India and Southeast Asia. Project Tiger concentrated its efforts on protecting areas of good tiger habitat, creating new reserves, and enlarging existing sanctuaries. The need for knowledge of the tiger's biology was left off the agenda for the time being. S. Dillon Ripley, then Secretary of the Smithsonian Institution, was one of a group of scientists who continued to press for a comprehensive study, arguing that it should be an integral and complementary part of any management scheme.

In 1973, after some discussion between the United States and International branches of World Wildlife Fund, the United States branch agreed to fund a three-and-a-half-year field study of the tiger. Royal Chitwan National Park in Nepal was chosen as the study site. John Seidensticker, who had studied mountain lions in Idaho, and Kirti Man Tamang, a senior forest official from Nepal, were recruited to begin the field work. After four years of negotiations, the project finally had funding, personnel, and support from an enthusiastic host government.

However, after only four months John had to leave, and the project ground to a temporary halt. It was at this point that Mel was asked to take over. Some of Mel's initial reluctance to accept the job involved the project's previous history. It was a high-profile study of an animal that had the world's attention. A lot of time, energy, and money had gone into the project already, and the Smithsonian and World Wildlife Fund (U.S.) needed to show results as soon as possible.

All the signs pointed to a healthy population of tigers in Chitwan, but the techniques for studying them had yet to be worked out. At that time radio telemetry was still in its infancy. Biologists had captured mountain lions with dogs in Idaho and darted lions from Land Rovers in Africa, but no one had yet tried capturing and radio tracking a big cat that lived in such dense cover. In this study it would be impossible to watch the tigers. All the data on the tigers' behavior would have to be collected by indirect methods such as radio locations, tracks, and other sign. Mel was well aware that reputations, his own as well as those of the project's major supporters at the Smithsonian, were at risk.

Mel arrived in Nepal in October and spent the first few months finding and negotiating the release of the project's equipment. He and Kirti made daily trips to the rather chaotic customs clearinghouse in Kathmandu, searching the ceiling-high jumble of boxes for signs of their vital telemetry gear. Between these daily customs pil-

The customs office at Kathmandu airport.

grimages they were kept busy obtaining a variety of permits and trying to locate suitable field vehicles. After a long search they finally found an ancient Jeep Wagoneer, a vehicle of great personality and not a few individual quirks.

Due only partly to its vivid paint job, this huge, heavy station wagon somehow acquired the name of "Green Latrine." It did about six miles to the gallon and held upward of fourteen people. There were no spare parts available for thousands of miles, so on several occasions local mechanics resorted to carving wooden brackets and struts to replace broken ones, just as they would have done for a bullock cart. The electrical system was a mess, and the tangle of jerry-rigged wires and tape probably contributed to its one major failing. It hated to start. The only technique that worked was for one person to sit in the driver's seat and jiggle the ignition key, while another person leaned under the hood and tapped on the starter with a hammer. If that failed, we pushed.

The other project vehicles were two young female elephants, who proved much more reliable and had better all-terrain capabilities than their mechanical counterpart. Finding properly trained elephants for the job turned out to be a complicated matter, and Kirti was invaluable during the search. He had hunted from elephant back and so knew what kind of animal was needed to work in the forest. He had also developed many useful contacts during his years with the Forest Department. The elephants had to be young enough to have a good working lifespan ahead of them, and they had to be female, because males are more difficult to work with and uncomfortable to ride. They also had to be accustomed to working amid the sights and sounds of the jungle. This last criterion was something Mel had not thought about until Kirti mentioned it, but it seems that elephants do forget. Many captive elephants spend their lives in the city, taking part in parades and ceremonies. They forget what the jungle looks and sounds like and need a long period of retraining and acclimatization before they can work there safely again.

After looking at dozens of potential animals, Kirti finally settled on two teenaged females, who became Smithsonian property for twelve hundred dollars each. They were named Kirti Kali and Mel Kali, Kali being the usual suffix for a female elephant's name in Nepal. They were a good investment, and unlike the jeep they doubled in value within three years. Later two more females, Prem Kali and Chanchal Kali, were added to the elephant stable.

While Mel was beginning work with the tigers in Royal Chitwan National Park, I was preparing to leave for Kathmandu. Although I had been born and raised in India, I had never been to Nepal before. The brief stopover in Delhi revived childhood memories, and my senses told me I was back in Asia. The colors of dawn are different. The morning air smells of dampened dust and spice. Visiting Westerners are often overwhelmed by the poverty and stench of the Indian subcontinent, but if you can teach yourself to see past these facts of life, there are glorious surprises in this ancient land.

Flying into Kathmandu, I could see the snow-covered Himalayas, shoulder deep in clouds. An old Nepali legend offers one explanation of how the mountains first came to Nepal. According to the story, all the mountains once had wings and flew about the world as they liked. However, the god of rain wanted to bring water to the people of Nepal, so he cut the wings from the mountains. The mountains fell to earth, and the wings became clouds, which still cling to the mountains. So wherever there are mountains you will see clouds, and the clouds will send rain to renew the earth.

Geologists say that these sharp, new peaks were born some forty million years ago in an epic collision of continents. India was then a separate continent drifting rapidly north into the larger landmass of Eurasia. As the two continents merged, the sea bottom that once separated them was forced up to form Tibet. Then the northern rim of India was pushed up into a second mountain range, which became the Himalayas, highest mountains on earth. From the air, the view is breathtaking, like watching geology in action. But once you have heard the legend, the clouds will always look like wings.

The city of Kathmandu was founded in the eighth century. Today it is a confusion of old and new. Air-conditioned hotels, four-lane highways, and electric trolley buses are juxtaposed with golden-domed temples, overflowing gutters, and houses without plumbing. Buildings and lifestyles spanning centuries are separated by only a few yards. In the older parts of town, the profusion of tiny shops and bustle of street vendors gave me the sensation of traveling in time. Despite appearances, there is a kind of organization among the maze of paths and alleyways. Clusters of shops are grouped by the commodities they sell: one street deals mainly in brass, copper, and aluminum cooking vessels; another in quilts and blankets; and another in beads and jewelry. The shops are tiny, not more than six by ten feet, and invariably full of people. In the street where fabrics are sold, saris and lengths of cotton cloth flutter outside the shops like colorful kites. On every side, mer-

chants display their most eye-catching wares, silks heavy with embroi-
dery or shot with gold and silver thread. Once you step inside a shop to
look, the proprietor or his assistant pulls roll after roll of cloth from the
shelves, unwinding them fast and furiously in dizzying waves of color.

Elsewhere in the bazaar, roving peddlers with pieces of cloth or
plastic laid out on the street sell flutes, sweetmeats, toys, and apples.
Beggars thrust their stumpy limbs at you, and loudspeakers selling lot-
tery tickets blare out inducements to buy. In the meat market there are
baskets of live ducks and chickens, nervous goats, and clouds of flies.
Sheets of mesentery dotted with globules of fat hang like curtains over
the windows, and goat heads shaved of hair and dyed orange lie among
cleaned and washed entrails. The intestines are chopped into inch-long
pieces, fried, and eaten as snacks.

*Temples near
Hanuman Doka
in Kathmandu.*

A street in the Kathmandu bazaar.

Around the Tundakel, or central parade ground, traffic is chaotic. Cycle rickshaws, motor scooters, taxis, and thousands of bicycles fill the air with noise and smoke, competing with street vendors and an army band. A sturdy shining bull pushes purposefully through the milling crowds, and a small boy tows a rope attached to a group of unwilling goats that are probably on their way to the meat market.

At night, the town closes down. Apart from foreign tourists and a few wealthy Nepalis, the streets are quiet. Mel had traveled to Kathmandu to meet me, and late one night after an evening out we set off to walk the three miles back to our hotel. Although it was not yet midnight, the town was deserted except for packs of small, shrill dogs. Each yapping pack ushered us to their territorial boundary, where we were met and similarly escorted by the next group.

Outside a luxury hotel, three boys wrapped in gunnysacks sat huddled round a tiny fire in the gutter. Seeing us, they leaped to their feet and began to whine, gesturing toward their stomachs, pleading for money in the internationally understood language of the hungry. They were comparatively lucky, for their beat was in a part of town frequented by plenty of wealthy tourists. Earlier in the day we had watched

the boys hawking trinkets, and they had defended their turf as assidu-
ously as the territorial dogs. We gave them some rupees and wished
them good night, feeling pangs of guilt as we left them to the cold,
empty street.

When we left for Chitwan, there was standing room only in the
domestic terminal of Kathmandu airport; half the town seemed to be
there, either waiting to leave or greeting arriving relatives. Tourists
clutching cardigans mingled with Sherpas and parties of trekkers. Behind the counter, harassed-looking officials made indecipherable an-
nouncements to the crowd: the weather was bad in the mountains and
all flights were delayed.

Westerners wait with great restlessness and fidgeting. They pace
the floor, consult their watches, and become irritable. In Asia, people
are much more expert. They have learned that the appointed time is
only a guideline and that becoming agitated serves no useful purpose.
When pressed by a foreigner for the exact time of an appointment or
meeting, Nepalis often suffix the answer with the words "Nepali time,"
meaning "roughly."

When our flight was announced, there was a rush for the door.
Passengers hustled across the tarmac toward the Twin Otter as if the
plane might leave without them if they were last in line. All twenty of
the plane's narrow plastic seats were occupied as we taxied lumpily to
the end of the runway. The stewardess offered cotton wool, green candy,
and sesame seeds. Everyone took handfuls of everything, and most
passengers soon had tufts of white cotton protruding from their ears.
At the end of the runway the pilot turned the plane and revved the engine until everything trembled and rocked. Finally the plane leaped forward, staggering erratically through the turbulent air.

Looking out of the scratched plastic window, we could see across
the entire width of the country. The plane cleared the ten-thousand-
foot Mahabharat Range with little room to spare. Millions of tiny terraces were carved into the steep slopes, giving the hills an unnatural,
orderly look. Now and then the white scar of a landslip showed against
the neat fields.

South of the Mahabharats a vast, flat plain stretched to India and
the horizon. This was the lowland portion of Nepal, famous for its forests and swampy grasslands. This was the land of the tigers.

We landed at a short, grass airstrip near the town of Bharatpur.
The small concrete building was half-painted yellow, as if someone had
run out of paint or energy midway through the job. Kancha Lama, the
driver, was waiting for us in the Jeep and didn't seem at all perturbed
that we were four hours late. We drove east, along the major east-west

highway through southern Nepal. The narrow tarmac road was covered with people, everyone carrying something—sacks of rice, bundles of wood, clay pots. Even the children were carrying other children. A truck covered with plastic bunting and pictures of wild beasts roared by. Its engine was hot and hammering, and the back was loaded with twice as

Terracing in the steep Mahabharat Range has allowed Nepalis to grow crops on every conceivable inch of soil.

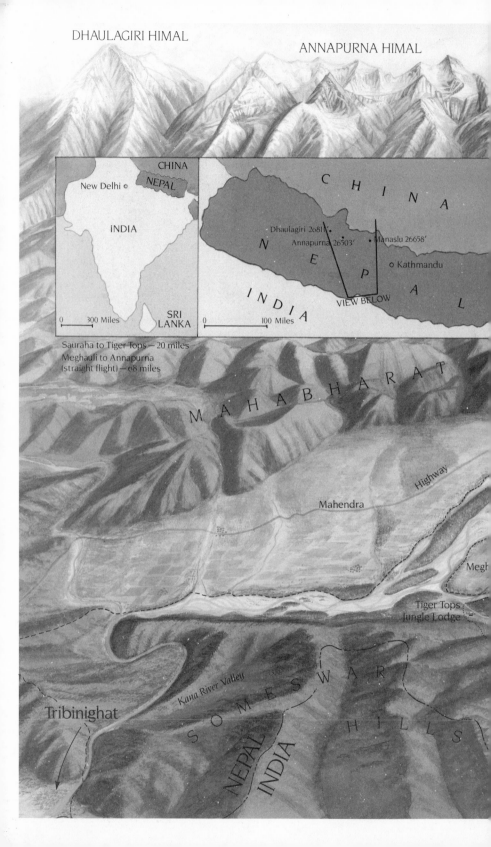

DHAULAGIRI HIMAL

ANNAPURNA HIMAL

CHINA

NEPAL

New Delhi

INDIA

SRI
LANKA

0   300 Miles

C H I N A

Dhaulagiri 26811'
Annapurna 26503'

Manaslu 26658'

Kathmandu

N E P A L

I N D I A

VIEW BELOW

0   100 Miles

Sauraha to Tiger Tops — 20 miles
Meghauli to Annapurna
(straight flight) — 68 miles

M A H A B H A R A T

Highway

Mahendra

Megh

Tiger Tops
Jungle Lodge

Kana River Valley

S
O
M
E
S
W
A
R

H I L L S

Tribinighat

NEPAL
INDIA

MANASLU HIMAL

nauli

H I L L S

Gorkha

Mugling

Kali Gandaki

River

Narayani

River

Naranghat

Bharatpur

Airport

Rampur

Tardi Bazaar

Our Camp

Bodrani

Sauraha

**Home Ranges of
Tigresses**

Rapti   River

Itarni Island

Sukhibar

Jarneli

Dudora Stream

ark

road

Kasra
(Park HQ)

Dumaria

Jaimangala
Village

Reu

C H U R I A

Royal Chitwan National Park

River

H I L L S

Madi   Valley

Map by Bob Eller Pratt

much as it should have been. Painted on the tailgate were the words "Good luck."

At the small town of Tardi Bazaar, a faded sign painted with the words "Royal Chitwan National Park" directed us down a dirt road. At a rocky ford, we crossed a river through wheel-high water, then wound our way through mud-and-thatch houses, tea shops, and haystacks. Orange pumpkins on vines trailed across the roofs of the houses, and geraniums and marigolds mingled with vegetables in tiny garden plots. Goats, cows, and chickens shared the road and forced Kancha Lama to drive at a walking pace. Even at that speed, clouds of fine dust poured into the Jeep like smoke, settling on everything. Even my teeth felt gritty.

Kancha Lama.

Chitwan, Nepal's first national park, was gazetted officially in 1973 by His Majesty King Birendra.

When Mel and Kirti first started work in Chitwan, they lived in a shaky wooden hut. By the time I arrived, the project had turned into a permanent camp with more than a half-dozen buildings. Quite luxurious in comparison with most field camps, our small, two-story house of wood, mud, and thatch grass had taken local carpenters two months to build. Upstairs there was a small office, a bedroom, and an open porch that ran the twenty-five-foot length of the house. The downstairs consisted of a combination dining room–storeroom. Beside the house was the bathing area, a six-by-six-foot, roofless, woven grass enclosure; fifty yards away, on the edge of the forest, was a small, thatched toilet hut. The kitchen was another small thatched hut with a mud hearth in which burned a wood fire. In characteristic Nepali tradition there was no chimney, so smoke from the wood cooking fire hung low in the room.

Although Mel had described the camp to me in advance, I was surprised to find it was so large. However, the two elephants alone were responsible for the livelihood of some fifteen people when wives and children were included. The elephants were essential, both for tiger captures and for getting around safely in the tall grass, but they were not cheap to maintain and required a large investment of time and manpower.

The Smithsonian–Nepal Tiger Ecology Project camp in Chitwan.

Our house in Chitwan beginning to take shape.

Each working elephant traditionally has three keepers. The *phanit*, or driver, is the senior of the three. He generally knows the elephant best and has the most control over it. Second in the hierarchy is the *pachhuwa*, who sometimes rides standing behind the *howdah*, or pad. Lowest on the totem pole is the *mahut*. In India, the order is reversed, and *mahut* is the title given to the most senior of the three elephant men. Both the *pachhuwa* and the *mahut* spend most of their time generally looking after the elephants, bathing them in the river after work, cutting toenails, finding the right kinds of food, and cleaning up afterward. All three men are closely involved with their charges, and at night the elephants are chained to large posts a few yards from their keepers' houses.

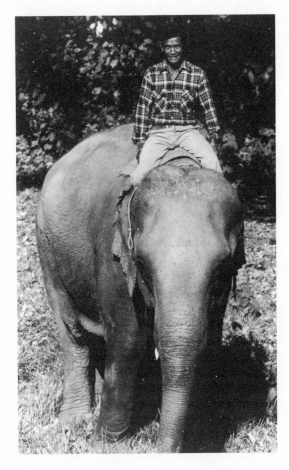

Bodai Tharu, *chief of the elephant staff, on* Mel Kali.

In addition to the elephants and their keepers, the camp was home to Kirti Man Tamang, who was studying deer; Kirti's wife Pat, an ex–Peace Corps worker; and their two boys, Kiran and Sonam. Kancha Lama (the driver), several *shikaris* (trackers), and Prem, the chief of *shikaris*, also lived in the camp compound. Prem was a skilled tracker and hunting guide, who in his youth had been associated with some of the royal hunts in Chitwan. Prem's intimate knowledge of tiger behavior and hunting techniques would help develop our method for capturing tigers.

Our nearest neighbor was Andrew Laurie, a student at the University of Cambridge who was studying Chitwan's population of rhinos for his doctoral degree. He had named one hundred seventy individual rhinos, identifying them by their scars, odd-shaped horns, and skin folds. We became not a little envious because Andrew could watch his study animals so easily, sometimes even from the porch of his small house on the riverbank. Despite this convenience, Andrew spent most of his time following his rhinos on foot or on elephant back, watching where they traveled, what they ate, and how they interacted with one another.

After only a few days in camp, it was obvious that our elephant transport was going to be a major highlight of the study. I spent hours watching the elephants and discovered that each one had a distinctly different personality. Kirti Kali was terrified of rhinos; if charged by one, she would turn her back, close her eyes, and pretend it was not there. Chanchal Kali was afraid of the dark but chased rhinos fearlessly. Mel Kali had a very sensitive nose for tigers and would stop to whoosh and mumble over a path that a tiger had recently taken. When she got close to a tiger, she trembled and shook with the deep belly noises of alarm that elephants make when they are uneasy or frightened.

Following a morning's work, the early part of the afternoon was set aside for elephant rest and relaxation, or bath time. It was an integral part of their daily routine, and the elephants seemed to know when it was time to head for the river. Once in the water, they cavorted and played like giant puppies, rolling over underwater, spraying each other, or totally submerging themselves in a joyful slow-motion ballet. After half an hour, the elephant handlers stripped to their shorts and joined their charges in the water. Shouting instructions to "stop that," and "roll over," each *mahut* carefully scrubbed his elephant until he considered her clean, then ordered the beast out of the river. Like children picking up their clothes after a swim, the elephants carefully collected their neck chains and carried them back to camp in their trunks.

We too fell into a daily routine. Mel and Kirti had already captured and radio collared two tigers, a leopard, and several deer before I arrived, and we spent the mornings searching for their radio signals

Tigress Number One, recovering from the tranquilizing drug after she was radio collared.

from elephant back. In the afternoons while the elephants had their baths, we walked or drove the Green Latrine in search of any animal we had not located during the morning. Signs of the tigers' presence were everywhere: scratch marks on trees, footprints or pugmarks on the road, alarm calls of deer, and sometimes the resounding roars of a tigress calling for a mate. We plotted the radio locations and all the other signs on a map and gradually felt as though we were getting to know the tigers as individuals.

The tigress known as Number One, because she was the first to be radio collared, lived just across the river from our camp. Number One was usually fairly easy to find, and we could often follow her nightly movements from the porch of our house. Sitting there in the dark listening to the soft blip, blip, blip of her transmitter, I could imagine her padding quietly along the trails near the river, searching for a meal. Each morning we scoured the sandy riverbank for her pugmarks and could usually piece together part of her night's activities by following her tracks. Sometimes there were flattened spots in the sand where she had crouched. Once, behind her body outline, a sweeping line like a snake showed she had flicked her tail back and forth in annoyance, probably at a herd of chital whose sharp hoofprints peppered the sand in front of her stopping place.

Another morning we found her pugmarks amid the milling tracks of a herd of chital in flight. A bloody place on the sand and a drag mark told us she had killed. We listened for her radio signal but she was not nearby, so we followed the drag into the tall grass. An area of flattened vegetation, more blood, elephant footprints and the tracks of men told the rest of the story. Number One must have made the kill at dawn, for we had heard the chital alarm calls just as it was getting light. She had dragged the carcass toward the safety and cover of the tall grass, but there had not been time to drag it far enough before the sun rose. Someone from the nearby government elephant camp on his way to collect forage must have seen her or read the tracks. Whoever it was had used an elephant to drive her off the kill and snatched it for himself.

The government elephant camp was about half a mile from our house. A relic of the days when the rulers of Nepal staged elaborate tiger hunts, it had once held scores of elephants. By the time we arrived at Chitwan, there were only a dozen or so left. Many of them, like the two tuskers Prem Prasad and Mote Prasad, were old and slow, but unlike our elephants they were unafraid of tigers. Several of the government elephants had taken part in the royal tiger hunts of the 1940s, carrying kings and heads of state. Driving a tiger off a kill was just harmless fun for these elephants and their drivers; some of them had been doing it for forty years.

A few days later Ram Lotan, head of the government elephant camp, came by to make amends. He knew we were annoyed at his drivers for stealing Number One's kill, and he offered to lend us one of his elephants for a tiger capture whenever we needed it. Mel accepted immediately, and we began to make plans to move to the other end of the park to radio collar more animals. I was finally going to see a tiger!

2   Catching a Tiger

*M*Y FIRST IMPRESSION OF preparations for a tiger capture was that it was somewhat like relocating a traveling circus. I marveled at the organization that must have been involved in the old-time tiger hunts, when three hundred or more elephants, their drivers, and scores of *shikaris* spent weeks in the remote jungles of the *terai*. For our tiger hunt, Prem and two *shikaris* set off in advance of the main group to put up temporary grass-thatch huts and start scouting the area for tracks and bait sites. Meanwhile, we assembled the huge mound of equipment and supplies for the capture operation. First there were the buffalos—we would need at least a dozen as baits to attract tigers. The buffalos would need two days to make the long walk to the campsite, so they would have to leave in advance with two people to accompany them. Mel Kali, Kirti Kali, and the government elephant could cover the distance in one long day but would have to travel light. Their rice rations, ropes, pads, and *pachhuwas* would have to be ferried to the campsite in a vehicle along with food, bedding, and petrol. Scales, a net to hold the tigers while we weighed them, and several hundred yards of white cloth known as *bhit* were also piled up to go. We would need to make at least three trips in the Green Latrine. Mel packed radio collars, tool kit, tranquilizing drugs, and telemetry equipment into two separate field kits to be carried on each capture attempt. Everything was checked and double checked, because once a tiger was darted there would be no time to run back for things forgotten.

On the day of the move the elephants left at three in the morning in an attempt to beat the heat. They would be tired when they arrived, for twenty miles in a day is quite a long trip for an elephant. We loaded the remaining equipment, Prem, Mel, Kirti, myself, three *shikaris*, and one of the elephant men into the Jeep, and after several stops to inspect tracks on the road and check for radio-collared tigers, we arrived uneventfully at the temporary camp near Sukhibar. Buffalos and elephants were already there, gear was piled everywhere, and some soldiers from the nearby guardpost had wandered over to have tea and join in the conversation. Grass huts, a kitchen lean-to, and makeshift benches and tables gave the place the air of a small village. It was difficult to believe it had all been put up in three days and would disappear without a trace after we left, but that was one of the advantages of Tharu grass-thatch architecture.

Prem had been working hard, walking the roads and trails in search of recent pugmarks and suitable places to tie out buffalos. The bait sites were very carefully chosen with a number of important criteria in mind. Obviously, they had to be in a place where a tiger would find them, so this meant locating all the main tiger trails in the area. Edges where forest and grassland met, major trail intersections, stream crossings, and deer trails were all ideal spots. But the baits also had to be in places where there was a chance of successfully darting the tiger once it had made a kill. They had to be near a patch of dense grass or bushes, because tigers prefer to eat their meals in seclusion and lie up afterward nearby. If there were no suitable retreats close by, the tiger might drag the buffalo a long way away or eat and leave, making a capture impossible. Finally, there had to be several easy-to-climb trees in the vicinity for us to sit in. This last requirement was the most difficult to meet, for sal, the dominant forest tree in Chitwan, usually grows straight and branchless for the first twenty feet.

For over a hundred and fifty years, tigers have been driven toward hunters waiting in trees. Tiger hunting in the Indian subcontinent used to be a common pastime of the wealthy and privileged, who relied heavily on the expertise of *shikaris* like Prem. Prem learned the art of tiger hunting from his father, who had worked as a royal *shikari* on the lavish hunts that took place in the *terai* during the 1930s and 1940s. The technique we used to capture tigers was a modified version of the "ring" hunt, invented in Nepal in the 1800s. The old method employed as many as three hundred elephants and even more men. Early in the morning *shikaris* would go into the jungle to examine the baits that had been tied out the previous afternoon. If one had been killed, they would quietly walk a huge circle, up to a half mile in diameter, around the site of the kill, bending the grass at intervals to mark a path that would form a ring. The elephants were then summoned and divided into two groups that proceeded to left and right around the circle like a pair of pincers, the rear elephants dropping out at intervals to station themselves along the boundary of the ring. When the two lead animals met, the order "Heads inward," was given. All the ele-

Setting out in the early morning to capture a tiger.

Mel radio tracking while standing on the hood of the Green Latrine.

21

phants then turned toward the center of the circle and moved inward, crushing the tall grass and tangled vegetation. The *phanits* whistled and shouted to drive the tiger into the middle of the circle. Finally the elephants stood shoulder to shoulder, the ring was complete, and the tiger was surrounded by a solid wall of elephants.

The stauncher elephants, carrying the guests of honor with rifles at the ready, would then enter the ring and move backward and forward, trying to catch a glimpse of the tiger in the dense cover. As many as four tigers were sometimes surrounded in the same ring, and the rumbling and trumpeting of the elephants, the excited shouts of the *mahuts*, and the roar of the cornered tiger charged the air with excitement. In his book *Big Game Shooting in Nepal*, E. A. Smythies cautions would-be participants that "this is not a sport for bad shots or hasty excitable people," and so it wasn't. In an effort to escape, tigers frequently charged the surrounding elephants, leaping onto their heads only to be shaken off again. Elephants often bolted in the face of such an onslaught, and people were thrown everywhere as terrified animals dashed through the vegetation. Many of the king's elite hunting elephants were trained to withstand a tiger attack and would flick the tiger off with a shake of their head and deliver a fatal kick with one powerful forefoot.

Over the years, it became more and more difficult to obtain the required number of elephants, and the ring drive was modified to include strips of white cloth known as *bhit*. The circle was delineated by this white cloth, and elephants were stationed at intervals behind it. Tigers tended to avoid the *bhit* cloth and thus could be kept in one place by only a few elephants until the guest of honor arrived.

Our capture attempts would be more modest and involve only three elephants and a dozen or so people. Rather than using a circle, we would lay out *bhit* cloth in the shape of a funnel. The people carrying dart guns loaded with tranquilizing drugs would be positioned in trees at the narrow neck of the funnel, while the wide end would be oriented to include the area where the tiger was thought to be lying with the bait kill. Once people were safely in trees and the cloth funnel was laid out through the vegetation, the elephants and *shikaris* would then move slowly through the four-hundred-yard funnel from the wide end toward the narrow neck. Coughing, shouting, and banging sticks together, they would try to drive the tiger slowly past the people in the trees with the dart guns. Prem said the tiger would take the line of least resistance, moving away from the noise and avoiding the cloth until it came out at the prescribed place.

However, Prem also maintained that darting tigers was far more difficult than shooting them. Unlike a rifle, the dart gun was only accurate within thirty yards, and to minimize the chance of hitting the tiger in a vital organ we could only dart animals in the muscle mass of the thigh or shoulder. This meant the tiger had to be close. The chances of

Laying out bhit *cloth during a capture attempt.*

Mel waiting in a tree at the end of a bhit-cloth *funnel with a dart gun.*

the right shot being available were slim. The tiger might not be resting in the clump of bushes where Prem thought it was; it might slip between the elephants and beaters; or it could come at a run, making a safe shot impossible. The tiger might emerge too far away or be screened by vegetation that would deflect the dart.

Most solitary, nocturnal creatures remained essentially unstudied until the early 1960s, when miniature radio transmitters were adapted for use on animals. Over the next ten years there were major improvements in batteries and waterproofing techniques, and radio tracking became more reliable and quite widely used. Today, radio transmitters can be made to fit almost any animal from a two-ounce bat to a thousand-pound polar bear, and the sophisticated electronics can relay a variety of information in addition to the animal's location, including body temperature, heart rate, and blood pressure.

Biologists are always concerned about the effects of a radio collar on an animal because no one wants to jeopardize an animal's chance of survival or study one that is behaving abnormally. For this reason, the general rule is that a transmitter should not weigh more than three percent of the animal's weight and the method of attachment should not restrict natural movement or activity. The transmitters we put on the tigers weighed about two pounds, or less than one percent of their weight, the equivalent of a collar on a pet dog.

Initially, most animals react to a radio collar in the same way that a domestic dog or cat might. They spend some time scratching, trying to get it off, and then become accustomed to its presence. All our radio-collared tigers and leopards made their own kills, mated, gave birth, and raised cubs. Some even returned to feed on bait kills the same day they were darted, suggesting that the procedure had few adverse effects on them.

The basic idea of radio telemetry is quite simple, but in practice it requires a great deal of experience to get the maximum information. Each small transmitter attached to an animal is built to operate on a different frequency, so in an extensive study there may be forty or fifty tagged animals, each of which can be "dialed up" by tuning the radio receiver to each animal's specific frequency. Signals are picked up by a directional antenna attached to the receiver. The antenna is rotated in a circle until the direction of the strongest signal is located. A compass bearing is taken in that direction, and then the researcher moves to another spot to repeat the procedure. This process, called triangulation, gives lines or bearings pointing to the animal. The bearings are plotted onto a map, and where the two lines cross is the location of the transmitter and, one hopes, the animal to which it is attached. It sounds easy, but in practice it takes a great deal of experience to discriminate where the strongest signal is coming from. Matters are further complicated by bounce, back and side signals, and dense, wet vegetation, which dramatically reduces the range over which signals can be detected.

On our second morning in Sukhibar, word came that a buffalo had been killed about a mile away and that there were tracks of a large male tiger at the bait site. The news caused a flurry of activity, half-empty cups of tea were abandoned, equipment and piles of *bhit* cloth were loaded onto elephants, and we were on our way. There was little conversation as the elephants hustled through the dripping fog; only the soft, scuffing noise of their feet and the clink of neck chains broke the silence. Everyone was preoccupied, wondering whether the tiger was still there and if so, how far it had taken the kill.

We stopped a short distance from the bait site, and Mel, Kirti, and Prem went in on foot for a closer look at the scene of the kill. Everyone else waited in silence. Any unusual noise might alert the tiger to our presence—even the sound of elephants feeding could cause it to leave, wasting the whole effort. Even under normal circumstances the elephants did not like to stand for long without eating. Now they seemed to sense the tension. Restless and uneasy, they shifted from side to side, their trunks reached out to grab bunches of grass or small branches, and their munching sounded incredibly loud in the silent forest. The drivers constantly murmured, "*Roh!* Stand!" and tapped them on the head with a stick.

The trail to the bait site led along the edge of a small *nullah*, or ravine. Tall grass and a mixture of stunted trees and brush covered one bank; on the other there was mature, open sal forest with an understory of waist-high grass and small palms. Shafts of sunlight angled through the morning fog, and condensation dripped from the leaves like slow rain. Mel and the others returned with the news that the tiger had dragged the kill into the forest. There did not appear to be many likely places where it could lie up, but Prem had seen some crows in a tree and wondered if they might not be watching the tiger. Crows often hang around tiger kills hoping for scraps. If the tiger had eaten and left, the crows would be on the ground feeding.

I looked around for a suitable tree to climb but there did not seem to be any; all the larger ones were straight and branchless. Even with the advantage of starting ten feet off the ground from the elephant's back, I would be hard pressed to find a branch within reach. Bodai, the elephant driver, knew how important it was to get people into trees quickly, and he grew more and more worried as we searched. Long delays increased the chances of the tiger hearing a noise or moving away. I saw that Mel had chosen his tree and was shinning up the straight trunk like a monkey, while Kirti had settled for a low branch only ten feet off the ground. Bodai pointed to a solitary silk cotton tree on the edge of a *nullah*, and I nodded. He murmured a command to the elephant and it leaned against the trunk, giving me a firm platform to start from. The first branch was just out of reach above my head, but I managed to scramble up and haul myself a few branches higher. Bodai smiled as he handed up my camera. The *shikaris* and elephant men were always amused by my climbing efforts, but until I came to Nepal I had never climbed a tree in my life. I tried to make myself as comfortable as possible and settled in to wait.

After half an hour the tree began to seem less than ideal. A thin line of ants marched up the trunk, heading straight for my trouser leg. Sharp, stubby spines dug into my back, and my right leg was completely numb. I wasn't sure where my feet were, and it seemed as though any slight movement would send me plummeting to the ground twenty feet below. Scores of tiny flies no bigger than pinheads buzzed a quarter of an inch from my eyes, never actually trying to land, just hovering. I closed my eyes for a moment and they left but soon resumed their irritating vigil. A breeze rustled through the trees, and a flurry of large sal leaves hit the ground with loud plops. Clouds of green parakeets swooped through the treetops, squawking loudly, and were gone. I wanted to move, to try and find a more comfortable position, but it was essential to keep completely still.

Mel had warned that the tiger could come at any time, five minutes after I had climbed into the tree or half an hour later. "If you don't move, it won't look up," he said. I felt alone and very vulnerable. My twenty-foot-high branch did not seem nearly far enough off the ground, and I glanced about for an escape route, just in case.

Suddenly there was a sound in the distance like an exaggerated cough, "Aaa-haa." Instantly other distant noises joined in; shouting, coughing, and sticks banging together. The beat had started. "Don't move, don't move," ran through my head, and I wondered wildly if anyone could hear my heart beating, it sounded so loud in my ears. I tried to raise the camera slowly to my eye to be ready to take a picture. Which path would the tiger take? Would I see it in time? The noise of the elephants and beaters grew louder and louder, and the *phanits'* voices rose in excitement. I could hear our elephant, Mel Kali, trumpeting madly.

A *shikari* stationed in a tree at the edge of the beat shouted, "*Bagh! Bagh ayo!* Tiger! The tiger's coming!" The elephant men yelled louder and faster, their cries tinged with hysteria. The elephants were rumbling, deep belly noises of uneasiness, lashing at the tall grass with their trunks. They were only a hundred yards away, and the tiger was somewhere in between. I scanned the grass in front of me. Which of three trails to concentrate on? Would the tiger come at a run, too fast for Mel to get a shot?

Suddenly! Unbelievably, like a whisper he was there. He paused, head and shoulders out of the tall grass, looked back, and opened his mouth in a noiseless snarl at the commotion behind. He moved unhurriedly out of the grass and down a thin trail that wound beneath our trees, dark gold, alert and confident, knowing he could easily outdistance the noisy elephants. He walked slowly under Mel's tree, and I could see the barrel of the gun following. Crack! A noise like a stick breaking, the gun fired. A loud woof! and the tiger was running, long loping strides up over a small bank and out of sight, the dry sal leaves rattling and crashing as he moved off into the distance.

The elephants were still thrashing around in the tall grass seventy-five yards away, their drivers unaware that we had darted the tiger. Mel pushed the button on his stopwatch to begin recording the time since the drug had been injected and waved vigorously to the elephant drivers. Finally someone saw him, and the commotion ceased.

The drug we used was CI 744, a combination anesthetic and tranquilizer especially developed for use on cats. It worked fast, had a wide safety margin, and unlike many other drugs on the market it was powerful enough to be effective in small quantities. This was important because it had to be injected into the tiger via a syringe dart fired from a modified shotgun, and the dart would only hold a teaspoonful of drug. We would have needed four times as much of any other drug for a large tiger, or more than one dart.

Whether a human or an animal is involved, anesthesia always involves a certain amount of risk. These risks increase outside a zoo or veterinary hospital because several factors are difficult to control in the wild. Excessive noise and disturbance are dangerous. Ideally, the tiger should be given a chance to move away and fall asleep without really knowing what happened. If the elephants continued the chase or people made a lot of noise, the tiger would fight the drug and end up further away and more difficult to find. We usually waited five minutes in silence before going after a tiger to give the drug a chance to take effect.

We were occasionally plagued by commercial film teams wanting to film the entire procedure, and they could not understand our reluctance to allow them to accompany us on these capture operations. Film teams are seldom small, and the very fact that someone is making a film attracts dozens of onlookers. Under these circumstances there is a real danger to the animal, for more people make more noise and disturbance, however hard they try not to. It is a thorny question for biologists, because films can help the public to understand the value of study, but if the filming jeopardizes the animal concerned, then the risk becomes unacceptable.

Our next problem was to find the tiger as quickly as possible. One of the few side effects of the drug was that it raised the animal's temperature slightly. That in itself was not serious, but Mel always worried that a tiger might become immobilized in a patch of sun and overheat before we found it. It was mainly for this reason that we limited our capture operations to the cool season, from November until March, and darted tigers early in the morning, before the real heat of day.

Searching for a drugged tiger was a nerve-wracking business. The clues were too small and subtle to be seen from elephant back, so the only way to find an animal was on foot. The vegetation was so dense that trackers would be almost on top of a tiger before seeing it, and because there was also a chance that not all the drug had been injected or that the dose might have been too small, a partially drugged tiger might be lying in wait.

I straightened my numb legs and looked at my watch. It was three minutes since the tiger had been darted. The elephants quickly made their way back to our trees, the *shikaris* and elephant men smiling and chattering, asking questions about the tiger: Did it run? How big was it? Did the dart stick? and the standard fear, Did it see you? Mel answered them, looking at his watch all the time, and I knew he was preoccupied with thoughts of finding the animal quickly.

"Okay, Prem, let's go," he said, and Prem rattled off a stream of orders to the *shikaris*. Two of the elephants disappeared to gather up the *bhit* cloth, and the *shikaris* collected tool boxes, net, scales, and other equipment we would need for the collaring operation.

Before I could climb out of my tree, Prem was already tracking the darted animal. Bent over the ground, he scuttled through the undergrowth like a mouse, occasionally waving a hand behind him when anyone got too close. Several times he crouched down and looked along the forest floor from an animal's viewpoint. He was looking for leaves that had recently been turned over, grass that had been bent and was springing back into place, all the minute details I could never see until he pointed directly to them. To watch Prem follow a trail was to observe the state of the art.

Kirti Kali, the elephant carrying the radio-tracking gear, followed ten yards behind Prem. She was hot after pushing through the tall grass and occasionally put her trunk into her mouth, sucked out some saliva, and sprayed it all over her chest and forelegs. The spray emerged with a whoosh and doused everyone nearby. Her driver muttered to her and tapped her head with his stick, not really trying to stop her but thinking he ought to seem to try.

After only a hundred and fifty yards, Prem stopped and pointed. Just visible through the vegetation was a patch of tiger fur. The black stripes and dark yellow background were perfect camouflage; we could easily have walked by ten feet away and not seen the animal. Now the question was whether the tiger was completely unconscious. There was no movement, but just to be sure Prem climbed onto the elephant's back and moved in for a closer look. "He's sleeping," he called.

The tiger was lying at the base of a large sal tree, his legs crumpled under him as if he had fallen asleep while running. What a truly awesome animal. His huge head with its distinctive individual markings rested on one forepaw, and the pure dark gold of his coat was incredibly clean. I wanted to touch his shining fur, but it seemed somehow irreverent to pat him as though he were an ordinary domestic dog. I felt as though touching him would be disrespectful, something I should only do under the guise of taking scientific data. I looked up to see Mel standing beside me. "Go ahead," he said with a smile.

The next few hours were filled with activity and anxiety. The *shikaris* cut a long pole, and we carefully loaded the tiger into a net and hung it from a spring scale. While Mel and five *shikaris* struggled to raise him off the ground, I read the weight from the gauge. He was a big animal, weighing four hundred and forty pounds, nearly beyond the capacity of the scale. I photographed his facial markings, the stripe pat-

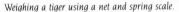

Weighing a tiger using a net and spring scale.

Kirti Man Tamang and Prem Bahadur Rai with Tiger 102.

terns on his flanks, and finally his huge feet. We examined his coat for parasites, monitored his temperature, and measured his teeth and body. It took two people to hold up his head while we measured his neck for the radio collar; it was the same size as Mel's waist.

As Mel was about to tattoo a number in the tiger's ear, he stopped in astonishment. "He's already got a tattoo," Mel said. Everyone crowded around. It seemed impossible, but the number 102 was quite distinct. That meant he had been the second tiger to be captured in the study. The 100 series were tiger numbers, and the 200 series were reserved for leopards, which we were also studying. Tiger 102 had been captured two years earlier by John Seidensticker and Kirti Tamang. Unfortunately the radio collar had fallen off soon after capture, but the tattoo was still visible. Tiger 102 was an extremely useful animal to have caught, and it would be interesting to monitor his movements in relation to the Sauraha Tiger who lived near our camp.

After everything was done, we moved Tiger 102 to a deeply shaded spot under a clump of small trees, cooled him with water, and propped him on his chest with his head on a pile of leaves and branches. After asking the elephants and people to move back, Mel and I sat down behind a tree twenty yards away to wait for him to recover from the effects of the drug. We sat quietly watching his respiration, Mel counting the number of breaths per minute and taking notes. It was all valuable information, because although tranquilizing animals is a routine veterinary procedure in zoos throughout the world, conditions in the wild are rather different. This was a critical part of the recovery period, when the tiger was particularly susceptible to disturbance. Enough of the drug had worn off for the tiger to be able to move a little and be dangerous, but he was still only partially awake. Noise or unusual movement could make the tiger stumble off and lie down in a less desirable place. He might collapse in a patch of sun and overheat or overexert himself trying to escape. We had no way of confining him to one place, so we had to rely on keeping disturbance to a minimum.

The day grew hotter and hotter. We were tired and thirsty and had left our water bottles on the elephants, but now was not the time to go in search of them. Nearby a common hawk cuckoo was screaming its call. Aptly nicknamed the brain-fever bird, it has an annoying three-

Prem tries to pour water on the half-awake tiger to cool him.

Mel and Fiona with Tiger 102.

note repertoire that it shouts over and over in a rising crescendo: "Brain fe-ver, brain fe-ver, brain fe-ver!" And then it begins again. I only noticed it when I was hot or tired, and then it was hard to ignore.

Five and a half hours after he had been darted, the tiger raised himself into a sitting position, looked around, then stood, ears forward, alert. I suddenly wondered if we shouldn't be in a tree rather than crouched behind one in case he noticed us. He walked in a large circle, looking quite awake and normal, then headed toward a small *nullah* where there was some water. We followed at a distance and watched as he crouched and drank for a long time. After surveying the surroundings suspiciously with his big golden eyes, he leaped the stream effortlessly and disappeared into a patch of grass.

We walked slowly back to the elephant waiting on the road. She was plucking trunkfuls of grass and stuffing the wads into her mouth, where they disappeared to the accompaniment of loud, hollow, crunching noises. The tension of the past hours had left us exhausted and drained, and although it was only mid-afternoon I felt an overwhelming desire to sleep. Back at camp there was tea waiting. The other elephants were out collecting fodder for their evening meal, and everyone was sitting around in the sun, quietly recovering. It had become a tradition to throw a party after every tiger capture, so Mel and I drove to the

Each tiger's facial markings form a unique pattern.

Tiger Tops Jungle Lodge to buy a couple of bottles of rum and tell Chuck McDougal our news.

Chuck is director of Tiger Tops, a luxurious tourist resort, and he has had a lifelong interest in tigers. He spends much of his spare time photographing them, following pugmarks, and studying tiger biology. Chuck has gathered a considerable body of information on the tigers living around the lodge, identifying each one by its distinctive facial markings. When a tigress appears at a bait site with cubs, he has a rough idea of when they were born, and he can record their facial markings for future use. Chuck looked at the Polaroid pictures we had taken of Tiger 102 and thought he recognized the animal. It seemed unlikely, but when he hauled out his photographic file, sure enough there was a match. Incredibly, Tiger 102 and an animal Chuck had called the Dakre Tiger were one and the same. He was the resident male near Tiger Tops, but Chuck had not realized that he ranged as far east as Sukhibar.

Chuck had first seen the Dakre Tiger as a large cub still with its mother in 1972. The next year he had begun to show up alone at bait sites. He was not independent but still used his mother's fifteen-square-mile home range. When he was three and a half years old, the Dakre Tiger began to make exploratory probes both east and west, and it was on one of these forays that he was first captured and radio collared. He was by then a sexually mature tiger in the unusual position of not

having to leave the area in which he was born. Young males almost invariably leave, probably because the adult resident male (their father)
becomes increasingly intolerant of their presence. However, for some
unknown reason there was no adult male in the area when the Dakre
Tiger had become an independent adult, so he was able to stay on and
become the resident male.

Armed with our new information, we returned to camp to find the
celebration in progress. Some *rakshi*, the local liquor, had appeared and
just as quickly disappeared into the *shikaris* and elephant men, who
were starting to relax after the day's tension and excitement. Someone
was singing, and the beat of a drum sounded through the camp. We
joined Kirti and Prem around the fire and over a drink told them what
we had just discovered about Tiger 102, the Dakre Tiger. It was astonishing that an animal about which we had known so little could
suddenly have a history. A major piece of information had been added
to our understanding of tigers with the capture of one male.

3   Chitwan, Then and Now

TO MOST OF THE world Nepal is exclusively high altitude, synonymous with massive snow-covered peaks, climbing expeditions, Sherpas, and yaks. However, only a third of the country is occupied by the high Himalayas. The cataclysmic merging of India and Asia also squeezed up two lesser ranges of hills. Closest to

The early morning sun catches the Himalayas, while the ten-thousand-foot Mahabharats are visible only as a dark line.

the Himalayas and just south of them is the ten-thousand-foot Mahabharat Range. A few miles further south toward India are the Si-
waliks, a mere geological wrinkle at three thousand feet.

The midland region of Nepal is a rugged, precipitous place. Over
half the country's population scratches a living from these geologically
young mountains, and the demand for arable land is so great that
people have laboriously carved millions of tiny terraced fields into the
steep hillsides. But terracing and deforestation are proving to be a lethal combination in these new mountains. Soil erosion problems are
staggering. Each year, Nepal loses as much as fifty tons of soil per hundred square yards of land. This is twenty times more in weight than the
amount of rice produced from a piece of ground the same size.

Until twenty-five years ago, the flattest, most fertile portion of
Nepal remained almost uninhabited. This lowland portion of the country, known as the *terai*, makes up a quarter of Nepal's land area and is an
unexpectedly different land of forests, tall grasslands, and swamps. Until recently, few people lived in the *terai* because of a combination of
malaria, inhospitable terrain, and a government policy of maintaining
the area as impenetrable forest.

In the mid-1700s a Jesuit priest named Father Marc journeyed
through the *terai* en route to Kathmandu. He wrote of tall grasslands so
extensive that it took three days to travel through them. A century later
the eminent botanist Sir Joseph Hooker, a contemporary of Charles
Darwin, described the *terai* in his journal as "supporting a prodigious
undergrowth of gigantic tall grasses that reached to our heads though
we were mounted on elephants." He added, "These gigantic grasses
seem to be destroyed by fire with remarkable facility at one season of
the year, and it is well that this is the case, for whether as a retainer of
the miasm [malaria] or a shelter for wild beasts . . . these grass jungles
are a serious obstacle to civilization."

Terai is a Persian word that means swamp. Rich alluvial silt de-
posits and a plentiful supply of water created a narrow belt of fertile
wilderness that stretched for over seven hundred miles along the southern borders of Nepal, Sikkim, and Bhutan. The *terai's* rich, subtropical
vegetation has always been renowned for its incomparable scenery and
diverse array of wildlife.

The swampy grasslands are shaped and nurtured by river systems
that carry snow meltwater and huge quantities of silt from the mountains. As the gradient becomes less steep and the water slows, some of
the silt load is deposited in a series of valleys called *duns* that divide
the Siwalik Hills, and also in the *terai* immediately to the south. Chitwan is one of these *dun* valleys. The national park lies in the southern

Elephant is the only vehicle that can penetrate the tall grasses.

The Rapti River, northern boundary of the park, clearly divides cultivated land from the forests and grasslands of Chitwan; the park is an island in a sea of farmland.

portion of Chitwan *dun* and is bounded on three sides by the Rapti, Reu, and Narayani rivers. Nearly three quarters of the park is surrounded by cultivated land and villages.

Until the beginning of this century, an aboriginal tribe known as the Tharu were the only inhabitants of the *terai*. They lived in simple, scattered mud-and-thatch houses and made their living by hunting, fishing, and raising a few crops. Somewhere along the way they must have developed a degree of resistance to the exceptionally virulent strain of malaria that existed in the region. Their way of life produced very few changes in the land, their numbers were small, and the forest quickly reclaimed abandoned settlements when their inhabitants moved on. In fact, the Tharu were part of the ecosystem.

Between 1846 and 1950, the ruling Rana regime maintained the *terai*, and Chitwan, as a private hunting preserve of the ruling classes. Severe penalties were exacted for poaching; anyone who killed a rhino was executed. However, those lucky enough to be invited to hunt there found Chitwan a sportsman's paradise. E. A. Smythies, who chronicled many of the royal hunts, called Chitwan "one of the most beautiful places on earth." He described the area as "saturated with tigers," and said that "rhinos were a positive nuisance."

During the cool, mosquito-free months of November through February, the Ranas hosted elaborate tiger and rhino hunts. Kings and foreign dignitaries were invited to take part in these extravaganzas, which involved months of preparations. Roads were carved through the jungle, luxurious hunting camps were built, and hundreds of domestic elephants were mustered to carry guests and round up the game. In a three-week hunt that took place in Chitwan in 1933, forty-one tigers, fourteen rhino, and two leopards were killed. Five years later, in the same area, Lord Linlithgow, the Viceroy of India, took part in a hunt that broke all records. In three months, one hundred and twenty tigers, thirty-eight rhino, and twenty-seven leopards were shot.

Despite these somewhat staggering body counts, preservation of the area as a royal hunting ground also preserved the wildlife. Hunts were held at irregular intervals and in different areas. The rulers of

*The central courtyard
of a Tharu village.*

Cattle graze in the stubble of fields that were once tall grassland.

Nepal had total control over a vast area of wilderness and could afford to leave large areas unhunted for decades. Despite the slaughter of tigers, the habitat and prey species were left intact and protected against intrusion, so the tiger population was able to recover between hunts. However, outside these royal hunting preserves the cultivation of the *terai* was already in progress. The wave of agriculture was soon to reach Chitwan, but until as recently as 1946 the valley contained over a thousand square miles of virgin forests, grasslands, and swamps.

In the 1940s the economic situation in the hill regions of northern Nepal steadily worsened. Overgrazing, deforestation, and overpopulation caused large-scale erosion and flooding. The Rana regime was overthrown by popular revolt in 1950, and the new government, obliged to look for areas in which to resettle displaced hill people, decided to open up the *terai*. An effective malaria eradication scheme, launched jointly by the United States Agency for International Development, the World Health Organization, and the Government of Nepal, was so successful that the *terai* was declared malaria free by 1960. It was open to all comers, and a migration took place that was unprecedented in the history of the country. Most of the *terai* was flat, fertile, and easy to clear. Forests provided timber and firewood for cooking fuel, and there was rich grazing for domestic stock. This new land must have seemed like a paradise to people used to scratching a living from the steep terraces of the hill region.

Within twenty years the *terai* was transformed into Nepal's granary, producing seventy percent of the country's food grains. The population of the Rapti River valley increased tenfold and two thirds of the Chitwan district disappeared under the plow. Hunting and poaching by the settlers were rampant, and little effort was made to control them. Swamp deer and wild water buffalo disappeared from Chitwan. Rhino were the main targets of poachers, and their numbers dwindled drastically. Wildlife was not alone in suffering during this large-scale influx of settlers. The peaceful Tharu were displaced by the more competitive hill people, who bought and bargained away the Tharus' land and destroyed forests that the Tharu traditionally had depended upon for their livelihood.

By the early 1960s, it was becoming apparent that something had to be done to turn the situation around. In Chitwan, a small force of armed guards known as the *Gaida Gasti*, or Rhino Patrol, was recruited to combat the poaching problem. Clashes between the guards and

Expanding populations and the demand for agricultural land have significantly reduced the forest cover of Nepal.

poachers resulted in casualties on both sides, but rhino numbers continued to decline. Finally a national park was proposed, but by then a multitude of settlements had sprung up in the area. In 1963 a government committee investigated the legal status of the settlers. A year later, twenty-two thousand people were resettled elsewhere in the Rapti valley. It was a brave and unpopular move that caused enormous resentment among the local population.

The old Rhino Patrol has since been replaced by over five hundred armed infantry troops from the Royal Nepal Army. The troops live in twenty-four guardposts, or *chowkis*, scattered throughout the park, and their presence has proved to be effective in controlling poaching and livestock encroachment. The soldiers are empowered to round up any cattle they find grazing within the park and impound them until their owners pay a fine to reclaim the animals. Under certain circumstances they are also permitted to shoot poachers on sight, an effective deterrent that has almost eliminated rhino poaching.

There is a strange beauty in the *terai*, not the dramatically alien quality of many exotic places but a soft mix of interwoven habitats that create a sense of richness without being oppressive. True tropical rainforest leaves me with a faintly disconcerted, claustrophobic feeling. I think it is the overwhelming sense of pushing, shoving, bellowing green. Huge, waxy shoots and leaves jostle one another in the airless, humid twilight, struggling for position in the mad sprint for the sky. The dense, crowded complexity stimulates the mind but stifles the senses; for me, it is too full. Most of the life and activity takes place up in the canopy, out of sight and reach, for that is where the light and food are. Only five percent of the sunlight that falls upon the canopy of a tropical rainforest reaches the ground, leaving the forest floor a dark, gloomy place of fungi, black shadows, and strange smells.

The subtropical deciduous sal forest that covers more than three quarters of Chitwan has a different feel. It does not crowd; the straight-boled trees stand separate and spaced, creating an open woodland. There are patches of sun and grass, scattered palms, and red-brown, castle-shaped termite mounds. The ground is dry and friable, covered with large, crunchy sal leaves. Rocks and stones roll out from under your feet as you walk, and steep *nullahs* dissect the hillsides. Remove the elegantly adapted sal trees that shelter the knotted mat of roots and grass, and the soil washes away in one short monsoon season.

Sal is the most common forest type in northern India and southern Nepal. It is a heat-, drought-, and fire-resistant tree that will not grow on waterlogged soil or recently deposited silt. In Chitwan, sal is

Intricately carved windows made from sal wood.

confined to the hills and better-drained portions of the valley floor. Although sal trees are deciduous, they are never completely leafless, and in spring the branches are laden with sprays of tiny, cream-colored flowers that fill the breeze with a faint perfume. Sal wood is strong, dense, and of great economic value. It is used for the construction of buildings, bridges, and railway sleepers. Most of the elaborate architectural carvings in Kathmandu are made from sal, as were the houses in our research camp.

The valley floor of Chitwan *dun* is a constantly changing mosaic of forest and grassland. During the monsoon, rivers tear away sections of forest along their banks, flooding grasslands and laying down acres of silt elsewhere. The rivers change course frequently, leaving abandoned oxbow lakes, or *tals*, that chart the waters' previous wanderings. Beds of dense, twenty-foot-high reeds surround these oxbows, inexorably converting them to shallow swamps, marsh, and finally grassland again. As the rivers recede after the monsoon floods, they leave a layer of fertile silt in the grasslands and create new mud flats and sandbars. These open areas are quickly colonized by a variety of grass species. If the new growth escapes the scouring of the next monsoon, a few years will see the open mud flats become tall grasslands.

Grasses stabilize the soil and create ideal conditions for tree species such as *sisso* and *khair* (a type of acacia). As young forests become established, grass is shaded out, and a dense understory of shrubs and herbs forms, creating the beginning of a belt of forest along the river course. This forest, commonly referred to as riverine, has the greatest plant diversity of all the habitat types in Chitwan and produces food for a variety of animal species. The dense understory also creates cover and den sites where many animals seek shelter.

Chitwan's mosaic of interfingering habitats and abundant water supply creates near-perfect conditions for its diverse fauna. It is a dynamic, rapidly changing ecosystem, created and maintained by the action of the rivers. Ancestors of modern grazing animals might well have evolved under conditions such as these.

Until the 1960s, Chitwan had one of the most diverse large herbivore faunas in the Indian subcontinent. It was the Asian equivalent of the African Serengeti. Large grazers like elephant, rhino, and water buffalo worked the swamps and riverine forests. Barasingha and hog deer were confined to the alluvial grasslands, while at opposite ends of the weight scale the small, primitive barking deer and the four-hundred-pound sambar lived solitary lives in the forest. Chital, or spotted deer, which graze and browse, exploited the glades and forest edges; and gaur, the primitive wild cattle of India, lived elusively in the densest forests. It must have been a naturalist's dream, an illustration of speciation and niche separation among large grazers rarely seen outside Africa. Although elephant, water buffalo, and barasingha are now gone from Chitwan, there is still an impressive variety of medium-to-large prey for tigers and leopards to feed on.

The barking deer is the smallest of the deer in Chitwan and takes its name from it distinctive alarm call. When danger threatens, it gives a short, sharp, single bark, "Arf!" like a hollow-voiced dog. It has a disturbing habit of moving around quietly, barking its single note like a ventriloquist so you never quite know where it is. Assuming that it responds to other potential predators in the same way, the technique may be an effective means of letting a predator know it has been seen, while the deer remains out of reach but close enough to keep an eye on the source of danger. Although all the deer in Chitwan have impressive alarm calls, it is the dimunitive, fifty-pound barking deer that seems to call first and fall silent last when a predator is around.

Barking deer are of great interest biologically because they have remained essentially physically unchanged for the last twenty million years. Presumably their behavior has not altered much either, so they give us an insight into how their fossil ancestors must have lived. A. A. Dunbar Brander, who was a forest officer in India for more than twenty

A *hog deer.*

years, described barking deer perfectly in his 1923 book on Indian wild-life: "When moving about the forest, they go at a slow mincing walk, picking their feet up into the air and placing these down again slowly and almost vertically." He also described them as "strongly place-bound," an observation our brief radio-tracking study confirmed. Two animals that we tracked for three months had very small ranges of thirty-eight and fifty-eight acres each.

Male barking deer have tiny, single-spiked antlers that grow out of a long, bony protuberance on the skull. They use their well-developed canine teeth for fighting and can inflict deep slashes on one another. Both sexes have large, gashlike glands just below their eyes, and they deposit scent from these glands on leaves and branches throughout their range. During his doctoral research on the deer in Chitwan, Hemanta Mishra found that barking deer live at low densities, mainly in sal and riverine forest. They are very selective feeders and spend most of their time browsing on tiny mouthfuls of leaves, buds, flowers, and fruit. Barking deer undoubtedly learn their small ranges well as they move around gathering these high-quality but thinly scattered foods.

Hog deer are slightly larger than barking deer and are the most primitive of the true deer (cervid) group. Their habitat requirements are extremely specialized, and they live exclusively in the alluvial grasslands of northern India, Nepal, and Burma. They have relatively short legs, and their hindquarters slope in the same hunched way as those of barking deer. Although the name "hog deer" derives from their piglike trotting gait, they remind me more of giant mice scuttling through the network of trails and tunnels in the tall, dense grassland. For most of the year they live alone or in groups of two or three, but after the annual fires they form small herds and emerge into burned, open areas to feed on young green shoots. Hog deer are quite numerous in Chitwan and are often killed by leopard and tiger.

Hog deer and the larger, more elegant chital belong to the same genus and occasionally interbreed. However, when you watch a hog deer sneak slowly through the dense grass or freeze when danger threatens, it seems much more similar to its forest-dwelling cousin the barking deer.

The lithe, lovely chital has been called the most beautiful deer in the world. The stags have long, graceful, three-tined antlers and weigh as much as two hundred pounds, while the slender, elegant does weigh

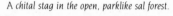

A chital stag in the open, parklike sal forest.

A *sambar, largest of the deer in Chitwan.*

about one hundred and thirty pounds. Both sexes have rich, brown coats permanently dappled with white spots. Grazers and browsers, chital are animals of the forest edge, emerging into glades and grasslands late in the afternoon. Like all the deer in Chitwan, they frequently give alarm calls when they sense danger. When a whole herd joins in, their wild, other-worldly cries echo through the forest like ghostly music. There can be few more ethereally beautiful sounds than chital whooping their short, high, flutey calls into the moonlight.

Related to the European red deer and North American elk, sambar are the largest deer in Chitwan and giants among the world's forest deer. Stags can weigh over five hundred pounds and does as much as four hundred. Despite their large size, they are amazingly difficult to see in the forest and resemble the shy, retiring barking deer in manners and behavior. It seems impossible that such a large animal should be able to hide so well, but we frequently approached within ten feet of radio-collared sambar before we saw them. During the day they remain silent and unmoving in their tangled beds of vegetation or sneak away quietly and deliberately.

Sambar are solitary or found in small groups of two or three,

Gaur, largest of the wild cattle. (Photo courtesy of Ullas Karanth.)

probably a female with her offspring of the previous year and a new fawn. They are more nocturnal than chital and prefer dense forests, where they feed primarily on leaves, shoots, and coarse grasses. Sambar does are often found day after day in a very small area. A female that we radio collared spent her days resting in a half-mile-square patch of riverine forest near our house. She was there almost every day for two years, and we rarely found her anywhere else. We could still recognize her by the colored tape on her collar long after the radio had stopped transmitting, and she continued to use the same tiny patch of forest until she was killed by a tiger six years later.

Apart from this diverse array of deer species, which so perfectly illustrates the adaptive radiation of the Old World deer in Asia, Chitwan has other large herbivores. Wild water buffalo disappeared in the 1940s, but gaur, the primitive wild cattle of Asia, still live in small herds in the undisturbed shadows of the hill forest. These shy beasts are rarely seen; the only traces they usually leave are the slim, pointed outlines of their hooves at a salt lick or on a riverbank. The occasional glimpses we got of them in their mysterious world had a magical quality, like watching a flickering old film of rare, uncatchable creatures.

Gaur have tremendous presence. The bulls are a shining, glossy black and stand five to six feet tall at the shoulder. They are eleven to twelve feet long and can weigh as much as a ton. Both males and females have heavy sweeping horns, and adults defend their young vigorously against predators: like musk oxen, gaur form a circle around their calves, facing out toward whatever danger threatens. With the abundant smaller prey available in Chitwan, tigers rarely kill adult gaur, but we did find the brown hair of gaur calves in tiger scats or feces.

Rhino calves also occasionally fall prey to tigers, but like gaur, adult rhinos are less vulnerable because of their great size. Indian rhinos are ponderous, prehistoric-looking beasts. They have thick, shield-like plates on their rumps and legs and a wrinkled, warty skin that folds deeply along the creases of their limbs. Indian rhinos have a decidedly ancient air about them and look like an older model of their smoother, more streamlined African relatives.

Chitwan is one of the only two places on earth where these rhinos still exist in the wild. The other is Kaziranga in the far eastern Indian *terai*. It is nothing short of a miracle that the Indian rhino survives at all, for if ever there were an animal destined for extinction, this would seem to be it. Hardly inconspicuous, the rhino lives only in the fast-diminishing swampy grasslands of the *terai*. It weighs several tons, is short-sighted and occasionally aggressive, relishes newly planted crops, and possesses a horn with supposed aphrodisiacal qualities.

A *greater one-horned rhinoceros.*

A wild boar drinking at a rhino wallow.

Rhinos are not difficult to shoot or trap, and females have only one calf every three or four years. Calves are born after a sixteen-month gestation period and weigh about two hundred pounds at birth, but their pink, premature-looking bodies and unformed faces hold only the vague promise of the eventual adult rhino.

There are a host of other animals in Chitwan besides these large grazers. We saw only tantalizing, fleeting glimpses of many of them, but they often recorded their night's activities in the soft dust of the roads and trails. Every morning the crisscrossed footprints on the road traced the previous night's animal traffic: three-toed, soup plate–sized prints of rhino overlaid with the sharp, stabbing hoofprints of a herd of chital; large, lacy prints of peacocks; the scuffle of a troop of macaques—all punctuated by the small neat feet of jackal.

4   Tracking the Tigers

RIENDS AND OFFICIALS WHO visited us could never understand how we managed to do what appeared to be the same thing day after day without growing weary of the routine, but for us, no two days were the same. When we were not tracking tigers, we were busy catching and following deer and leopards. Because the tigers' movements and behavior patterns were influenced by the nature of the animals they preyed upon, we needed to know something about the deer. This was Kirti's project, and he had radio collars on four different deer species to establish where they fed and rested, when they were active, and how important the different deer species were in the tigers' diet. It was also important to figure out how tigers and leopards differed with regard to diet and habitat use, and this required putting radio collars on several leopards in the area. We monitored all these animals in much the same way as we did the tigers.

Every morning we set out early on the elephants, searching for radio-tagged animals. In the afternoon, while the elephants grazed and rested, we went out on foot to locate animals that lived closer to camp. On those occasions when the Green Latrine could be persuaded to run, we drove the length of the park looking for animals that ranged beyond areas we had checked on our morning rounds.

The three seasons dictated their own changes in this routine. From November through February, winter brought clear, warm days with cool, almost frosty, nighttime temperatures. After dark, a heavy ground fog blanketed the vegetation, and by morning the air was saturated and moisture dripped like rain from every surface. Going out first thing on the elephants meant being showered with water from trees and tall grasses, and we were usually soaked and cold until ten in the morning, when the fog burned off and the temperature rose. Then the air was clear and crisp, cleansed of smoke and dust, and every detail of the Himalayas was sharp and magnified.

In summer we were up by four-thirty, drinking tea in the quiet half-light of dawn. Afternoon temperatures were frequently greater than one hundred degrees Fahrenheit, so we tried to do as much as possible in the mornings, both for our comfort and for the sake of the elephants. Any temptation to linger too long over a second cup of tea was thrust aside by the sounds of the elephants waiting patiently outside. As if to remind us that it was time to get going, they shuffled their feet and whooshed gently through their trunks. It was much easier to procrastinate on days when we were using the Jeep.

An integral part of the daily routine involved a stop in mid-river to let the elephants drink. Early-morning mist swirled pink and gray above the steel-colored water, creating a landscape without horizons, sky and water merging in a gauzelike blur. The elephants burbled and slurped as they stood belly deep in the water, siphoning gallon trunkfuls down their throats. Thirst quenched, they dawdled like children, making unconvincing attempts to persuade us they were still drinking, then briefly snaked their trunks across to one another's mouths in elephant conversation. The drivers signaled an end to the refreshment stop, and the beasts grumbled but obeyed, moving forward across the

Mahuts preparing the elephants for an early morning trek.

Heavy winter fog shrouding our camp.

river. In places the water was halfway up their bellies, and the elephants reached their trunks ahead as if sounding the depth of the river in front of them.

Crossing the Rapti River in the monsoon season was a different matter. We frequently had to wait several days for the water to recede to a level that was safe for the elephants. From June till late September, southeasterly winds sweeping up from the Bay of Bengal bring heavy rains; as much as one hundred inches fall in these four months. Rivers rise ten feet or more, and extensive areas of the floodplain are inundated for weeks at a time, making it impossible to ford the Rapti River in the Jeep, and crossing on elephant back dangerous. The current is swift and strong; brown, boiling water carries trees, branches, and other flood debris hidden in its swirls.

On days when the water looked low enough, we inched the elephants gingerly across, watching nervously for floating logs and trees. The river crossing was some two hundred yards wide, and the drivers headed their elephants upstream so that they angled into the strong current. Bodai told us it could be fatal if a driver allowed his elephant to be turned broadside to the full force of the river, and I thought about his warning every time we crossed. There were times when we could feel that the elephants' feet were only occasionally touching the river bottom. We clung to our equipment and the ropes of the elephant har-

55

ness while our incomparable, all-terrain vehicles bumped and bobbed across the turbulent water like heavy corks. It sometimes took almost an hour to make the crossing.

On one occasion the force of the river proved to be too much for one of the struggling elephants. Kirti Kali's driver failed to keep her facing upstream, and by the time he realized he was in trouble, it was too late. He shouted commands and kicked at Kirti Kali as he felt her body turning broadside to the current, but she could not respond. We watched in horror as the full power of the river slammed into Kirti Kali's body and lifted her off her feet. She swam for a few seconds, then disappeared in a swirl, as if a giant fish had swallowed her. Twenty yards downstream she reappeared, feet in the air. She rolled over and went down again, but this time her trunk came up and stayed above the surface. Bodai, who was driving our elephant, shouted angry instructions to Kirti Kali's *phanit* while he tried to maintain his own elephant's balance in the whirling water. He was furious with the driver, who he said had not been paying attention to the river.

Kirti Kali managed to right herself eventually and made it back to the bank, but by the time she reached dry land she had been swept more than half a mile downstream. The two people on her back survived by clinging to her harness, but the radio-tracking equipment was soaked and ruined. Back in camp, we unscrewed the top of the receiver and poured the water out of it, remembering the manufacturer's instructions to "keep the instrument dry and free from humidity at all times."

Even when elephants didn't capsize, work was most difficult in the rainy season. The monsoon rains triggered frequent hatches of locust-like insects that ate our notebooks, clothes, and anything else they could get to. At night our lanterns attracted clouds of stink beetles, and we ate our evening meals with the aid of two plates, using the second to cover the food between mouthfuls. High humidity and rainfall played havoc with the electronic equipment, and to keep cameras and radio receivers functioning we stored them in air-tight containers filled with silica gel. The coarse crystals absorbed moisture but had to be heated regularly to maintain their effectiveness, so part of our daily routine involved cooking pounds of silica gel in a frying pan.

Our daily elephant trips through the forest and grassland gave us brief glimpses into the lives of some of the other wildlife in the area. Loud, sawing wingbeats announced the approach of a group of giant hornbills flying low over the canopy in search of fruiting fig trees. They seemed to favor one particular patch of forest, and we

Mel examining pugmarks
on the park road.

rarely saw them anywhere else. The hornbills' forest, one of my favorite places, was distinguished by a tall, bushy plant that did not grow anywhere else. The plant had green-black leaves and seemed to be in flower year-round; its white, periwinkle-like blossoms perfumed the air with the heavy scent of gardenias. Even at noon the hornbill forest was cool and fragrant, like an enchanted cave. The sambar and wild boar liked it too, and we often found them resting there in the quiet green gloom.

Once a small striped piglet, separated from its mother, came dashing down the trail toward us. Kirti Kali stopped, moved her feet up and down nervously, then stretched her trunk out to sniff it. Not liking its beetlelike quickness, she slammed her trunk on the ground and growled. The piglet stopped and peered. Kirti Kali shuffled her feet again and screamed. Hit by the blast of sound, the piglet turned and bounced off through the forest, calling for its mother.

One morning during a routine search for our radio-collared animals, we found the pugmarks of a tiger. The tracks must have been

When we darted the Sauraha Tiger we were amazed by his great size.

made earlier the previous evening, for they were blurred in places by the comings and goings of other night animals. The size and shape of the tracks suggested it was a tigress, probably Number One.

Mel and Prem got off the elephant to follow her long, deliberate strides more closely, while I scanned our surroundings with the antenna, hoping to pick up a radio signal. Every fifty yards or so the pugmarks showed where the tigress had detoured from the road to spray urine, and over a distance of two miles we found seventeen places where she had scent marked trees or bushes at the side of the road. Her tracks left the road and turned onto a rhino trail through the tall grass. The path ran along the edge of a patch of forest, where the abrupt transition from tall, marshy grass to trees marked an almost-filled-in oxbow lake. At the edge of the water, against a background of bronze grass canes, three otters, one with a shining fish in its mouth, stood on their hind legs to watch us pass.

As our elephant climbed the small steep bank into the trees, the driver murmured words of advice to her about stumps and low branches. "Dek! Look!" he said, and the elephant did, carefully lifting her feet and holding branches aside with her trunk so we wouldn't be scraped off her back. The radio signal grew stronger, and we quietly circled the dense thicket Number One had chosen as her rest site for the day.

All the signs suggested that Number One had finally come into estrus again after a two-year hiatus. Her two cubs no longer needed her to kill for them, and she would soon mate and give birth to a new litter. If we kept track of her movements, we should be able to discover who would father her next litter.

We found Number One's independent daughter, the Roaring Tigress, resting near the river about a mile from her mother, and we then went on in search of the male cub known as 104, who was the Roaring Tigress' brother. Although he was only twenty-four months old, he moved over a much larger area than his sister and was often difficult to find. We knew Tiger 104 would soon take off in search of his own home range and were anxious to keep track of his movements.

The morning was heating up as we headed toward the center of the park. Colors that had been vivid and shining earlier in the day now took on a dusty, flat look, and the air shimmered and wavered with heat. Iridescent jungle fowl males and their escort of dun-colored hens scratched and danced in piles of rhino dung along the road, dashing off into the bushes when we got too close. The elephants were hot and irritable, annoyed by inch-long, blood-sucking insects that looked like giant horseflies. These flying hypodermics have mouthparts powerful enough to pierce an elephant's skin, and they made short work of us.

However, they were sluggish fliers, easily caught and quickly dispatched with a satisfying pop.

Riding an elephant during the heat of the day is an excruciatingly slow and painful experience. When elephants are tired and hot they seem to creep along, and their riders lurch and roll, backward and forward, with every ponderous step. We got off and walked ahead of the slow, shuffling beast. Just as we were debating whether to return to camp, another set of pugmarks appeared in the dust of the road. There was no question as to whose they were; size alone told us they belonged to the six-hundred-pound Sauraha Tiger. He was the territorial male at the Sauraha end of the park, and his range encompassed the areas of at least three females, one of whom was Number One. He was almost certainly the father of the Roaring Tigress and her brother Tiger 104 and the most likely candidate to mate with Number One this time.

Grateful for the chance to follow his night's activities for once, we backtracked along his huge pugmarks. Despite intensive searches, we had not heard his radio signal for a week and were anxious to know where he had been in the interim. The pugmarks strode straight down the road toward us, never stopping or deviating from the path. The Sauraha Tiger had obviously been more interested in traveling than hunting the previous night. After half an hour of backtracking along his trail, we decided to turn around and find out where he had chosen to rest for the day. We would return later in the afternoon in the Jeep for the longer task of discovering where he had begun the night's travel. We found him near an oxbow lake named Majur Tal. Less than a quarter of a mile away, but also near the water's edge, was Tiger 104, brother of the Roaring Tigress. It had been an excellent morning—it wasn't often that we found four tigers in a day.

By persistently following the tigers day after day, using the signals from their radio collars combined with pugmark tracking, we gradually built up a picture of their social organization. Patterns emerged slowly, but toward the end of the first year we felt we were beginning to understand how these elusive predators lived. The first thing we discovered was that Chitwan tigers rarely spent two consecutive days in the same place. This may not seem like a great revelation, but it was extraordinarily useful: if we could manage to locate each tiger every day and link tracks on roads, trails, and riverbeds to specific individuals, then we could map each tiger's nightly movements in relation to its neighbors.

There were not enough hours in each day to do all of these things, so to begin with we concentrated on females, who were easier to follow.

Later, by incorporating Chuck McDougal's information on tigers at the other end of the park, the pattern of male ranges became clear. It was obvious that home ranges, while fulfilling the same basic function for the two sexes, meant different things to males and females.

Tigresses established and maintained relatively small, exclusive home ranges in which they hunted and raised their cubs. Most tigresses living along the prey-rich floodplain had small ranges of six to eight square miles. When we plotted the ranges on the map, they looked like beads strung along the thread of the Rapti River. Water, suitable den sites, and sufficient prey were the primary factors that concerned tigresses. They needed to be able to regularly and predictably find and kill enough food for themselves and their growing cubs.

Males, on the other hand, had different priorities. Their ranges were from two to seven times as large as those of females and obviously contained more than enough food, water, and den sites to satisfy their needs. Although each male's range overlapped several female ranges, they butted up against but never overlapped the ranges of neighboring males. There are a few reports of overlapping male ranges

A *tigress resting in a* nullah.

from other parks, but without knowing the males' backgrounds such information can be misinterpreted. For example, the Sauraha Tiger tolerated his not-yet sexually mature son using his territory. Since the son, Tiger 104, was large enough to be classified as fully adult, we could easily have assumed they were two unrelated adults males amicably sharing a territory. Basically, females compete among themselves for access to resources like food, and males compete for access to females with which they can mate and sire cubs. Each sex is doing all it can do maximize its chances of leaving as many offspring as possible—the definition of success in biological terms.

Environmental conditions, the availability of key resources, and territory size vary considerably over the tiger's broad geographical range. However, like most cats, the tigers' different spacing patterns are simply variations on a common theme. The territories of females may be small and exclusive, as we found in Chitwan, or as large as one hundred twenty to one hundred sixty square miles and widely overlapping, like those of tigresses in the Soviet Far East. Male territories may encompass the territories of one or several females and be as large as four hundred square miles. Territory size is influenced mainly by the abundance and distribution of prey and whether the prey migrate seasonally. Thus it is not just how much food there is but whether or not it is available throughout the year. In Chitwan, deer and wild pigs are abundant and stay in the same area year round. In the Soviet Far East, where wapiti and other prey species migrate over long distances to winter feeding areas, the tigers follow their prey; their large ranges are simply reflections of changes in prey availability.

In the afternoon, while the elephants grazed and rested, we drove out to continue following the Sauraha Tiger's tracks. They were difficult to see, and there were long stretches where they had vanished beneath the day's animal traffic. While Mel walked ahead, I followed slowly in the Jeep, almost suffocating under the cloud of soft dust that poured through every crack of the vehicle. To my great relief, the Sauraha Tiger's tracks turned off and disappeared before we reached the park headquarters at Kasra. We took a side road to Lami Tal, a nearby oxbow lake that was a favorite haunt of tigers. It was a guessing game, trying to anticipate which of several routes the Sauraha Tiger might have chosen to travel from one end of his range to the other.

There were no tracks at Lami Tal, and as Mel tried to locate a radio signal, I washed my face and hands in the stagnant water, trying not to think about the rhinos that used it as a bathing place. Coots and purple moorhens paddled around clucking and chattering, while a party of

Mel listening intently for a radio signal.

open-billed storks stared down from the trees above, waiting for us to leave so they could resume their probing in the mud for snails. Anxious, red-wattled lapwings circled, screeching their raucous "Did-he-do-it" chant, and a tiny, metallic-blue kingfisher sped by like a miniature fighter plane, only an inch above the surface of the water.

At dusk, we picked up the Sauraha Tiger's pugmarks again just west of Kasra, a straight-line distance of at least six miles from where we had found him resting earlier in the day. Another time we had tracked him for eight miles along the main park road. We were particularly interested in the Sauraha Tiger's long trips because they were uniquely male; tigresses rarely made such long, direct moves.

Tigers maintain their ranges and conduct their social lives with a combination of visual signals, scent marks, and vocalizations. Both males and females deposit scent marks throughout their ranges at all times of the year. They also make scrapes by raking the ground with their hind feet and leave feces in prominent places along roads and trails. No one has been able to figure out exactly what information these marks convey to another animal, but it probably includes individual identity, sex, reproductive condition, and the time the mark was made. All this information is deposited along a network of commonly used trails to indicate that an area is occupied and that within that marked area certain rights and privileges are claimed by the marking animal. The marks do not necessarily exclude other tigers; we occasionally noticed transient animals passing through occupied areas. However, these visitors never stayed long, suggesting they may be at a disadvantage. Resident tigers who have been neighbors for some time probably come to know each other by sight, sound, and smell. They have probably resolved their difference and waste little time and energy in hostile exchanges.

Scent marks and long-range calls also serve to bring animals together for mating purposes. When not accompanied by dependent

A male tiger chin rubbing on a tree.

cubs, tigresses come into estrus every fifteen to twenty-five days. However, as they are probably receptive to a male's advances for only two or
three days of each cycle, the male must be able to find the female at
the right moment and time his visits to coincide with her peak of recep-
tivity. Studies of tigers in captivity suggest that tigresses increase the
frequency of scent marking just before they are ready to mate, and it
seems logical to assume that they thus give males a better chance to
locate them in time.

Male tigers then must visit most parts of their ranges regularly to
ensure that they detect estrous females. Because scent marks fade,
both males and females must also revisit and remark all portions of
their ranges at regular intervals. Thus we felt the long, rapid movements of the Sauraha Tiger were related to renewing his scent marks,
checking on neighboring males, and assessing the reproductive condition of tigresses in his area.

We returned to camp in the evening, and after a bath from a
bucket of warm water, we spent an hour on the porch en-
joying the predictable sights and sounds of approaching night. The
birds seemed to take turns, species by species, to go to bed. First the
late-afternoon cheeping of thousands of dusty house sparrows faded
to silence, then kinetic mobs of squawking green parakeets flew over on
their way to roost in high trees in the villages. The elephants rumbled and
shook their chains, impatient for their evening meal of rice and molasses
balls, imploring passersby with outstretched trunks. In the brief interval
between sunset and darkness, when it became difficult to see, groups of
pond herons settled into a tree opposite the house, always into the
same tree and always with the same deep staccato "Awk, awk, awk"
squabble over perching places. Most evenings a sleek, nut-brown jungle
cat emerged from the forest onto the path that led from the river. With
silent, precise steps it picked its way across the compound, stopping
occasionally to listen to the sounds of people. It was on its way to the
village, probably to hunt mice, rats, and unwary chickens.

While the sun had set for us at sea level, it continued to light up
the twenty-thousand-foot peaks of the Annapurna Range. The last rays
of the sun etched each detail of the peaks in deep pink and magenta;
as if to remind us of their greatness, they alone were illuminated while
the rest of the world lay in darkness. It is not difficult to see why the
Nepalis regard the mountains as gods.

After sunset, if the nights were cold, we gathered around a fire
built outside in front of the house. At some point during the evening a
distant jet would rumble through the clear, bright stars—the seven

Bodai and a helper making up elephant rice balls.

o'clock flight to Delhi, always late. Evenings were a time to talk over the day's radio-tracking results with Kirti, Pat, and Prem and resolve disputes among the staff. There were always major or minor ongoing crises: a loan needed before the next payday, a ride to the health clinic in Bharatpur, or medicine for a sick child. We had a well-stocked first-aid kit and could treat common ailments, but any serious illness meant evacuation to Kathmandu. Other nights, we sat indoors in the office with a kerosene lantern, analyzing data, writing reports, or reading. Mel taught me to play poker, and we bet heavily with matchsticks and paperclips.

Like most people who live without electricity, our routine was dictated by the daylight hours. In winter it was too cold to stay up late, and in summer we had to be on our way by daybreak to avoid the heat of the day, so we were usually in bed by nine-thirty. Rhinos were frequent nocturnal visitors to camp and often used the main support beams of our house as scratching posts. Their presence made late-night trips to the toilet quite a production, and after being cornered in the flimsy outhouse once too often, I insisted that Mel stand on the porch with a flashlight to make sure nothing was lurking nearby.

Nights were rarely silent in Chitwan, and we were lulled to sleep by the mixed sounds of forest and village. Next to our house the elephants rumbled at phantom leopards, eliciting drowsy shouts of "E*eee hathi!*" from their drivers. Village dogs barked, and farmers in the fields shouted to drive deer and rhinos from their crops. Out on the floodplain, distant alarm calls of chital marked a tiger's progress through the grasses.

5   The Mauling

*M*ORE THAN ANY OTHER predator, the tiger has become a symbol of power, strength, and untamed wildness. For centuries tigers have inspired art, legend, and literature, and great metaphysical powers have been attributed to various parts of their bodies. In many Southeast Asian countries, the tiger is considered to be the King of Beasts, and people believe that the courage and strength of the animal is passed on to those who eat its liver or flesh. Contrary to popular belief, the bones, claws, whiskers, and internal organs are valued far more highly than the tiger's skin, and an array of poisons and patent medicines is brewed from the animal's body parts. The fat is prized as an aphrodisiac, and tiger whiskers can either kill a man or make him potent, depending on whether he lives in Malaysia or Indonesia.

The tiger has generated a mystique quite unlike that surrounding other large cats. Even lions do not evoke quite the same feelings of terror and awe. Given that both cats are similar in size, and apart from coat patterns, not all that different in appearance, why should people feel so differently about them? Perhaps because lions are more visible as they go about their daily business, they are somehow less frightening. The tiger's solitary lifestyle and intimate connection with darkness may be partially responsible for the difference. Certainly the fact that it is almost impossible to see tigers in their natural habitat only adds to the mystery. Even experienced hunters like Corbett, Forsyth, and Sanderson, who spent much of their time in the jungle, wrote of how rare it was actually to see a tiger. "During ten years of pretty constant roaming about on foot in the most tigerish localities of the Central Provinces, I have only twice come across a tiger when I was not out shooting," wrote Forsyth.

Although the tiger itself is seldom seen in the wild, signs of its powerful and deadly presence are more obvious in the alarm calls of nervous deer, pugmarks at waterholes, or the deep, moaning roars of a tigress. Somehow the tiger's invisible, unchallenged power touches our deepest fears of the unknown.

The tiger is not the only big cat that preys upon humans, but it does seem to do so more regularly than lions, jaguars, or leopards. The fact that tigers do occasionally include humans in their diet must be the major contributor to their larger-than-life image. Indeed, the vengeance of a dead tiger is universally feared, and villagers frequently denied any knowledge of a tiger's presence in their area when questioned by Western hunters. In many parts of India and Southeast Asia, people believe that the ghost of a man-eating tiger's last victim chooses the next person to be killed. According to legend, the ghost rides on the tiger's head and points out anyone who has betrayed the tiger's movements.

The literature is full of examples of the tremendous number of victims each man-eater managed to claim before it was finally dispatched. In 1769, man-eaters reportedly killed over four hundred people in the area of Bhiwapur, India, and caused the town to be abandoned. By 1907, the Champawat Tigress had killed more than two hundred people in Nepal and was driven over the border to India, where she claimed another two hundred and thirty-four victims. When Jim Corbett arrived to deal with this man-eater, he found an entire village inside their homes behind locked doors. No one had been outside for five days, and the tigress was roaring on the road a few hundred yards away. The tigress killed another two people before Corbett managed to shoot her.

Historically some geographical regions seem to be more prone to man-eating problems than others; man-eaters are rare in south India but common in the Sunderbans of Bangladesh and India. The Sunderbans is four thousand square miles of tidal creeks and mangrove forests that contain the world's largest single population of tigers. Few people live there, but men and women do enter to harvest firewood, honey, and fish. The area has been notorious for its particularly bold man-eating tigers for more than two hundred years, and stories of tigers climbing into boats and galloping along the riverbank after a canoe full of people have been authenticated. The problem has by no means disappeared, and in the Indian Sunderbans alone authorities have officially recorded four hundred and twenty-nine deaths resulting from tiger attacks in the last ten years.

In general, however, attacks by tigers are rare. A hundred times more people are killed each year in India by snakebite than by tigers. Tigers prefer to avoid people and usually give them a wide berth. Even when pressed, they will normally give a warning growl and allow the intruder to back off gracefully. As Jim Corbett so aptly wrote, "Tigers, except when wounded or when man-eaters, are on the whole very good-tempered. . . . Occasionally a tiger will object to too close an approach to its cubs or to a kill that it is guarding. The objection invariably takes the form of growling, and if this does not prove effective it is followed by short rushes accompanied by terrifying roars. If these warnings are disregarded, the blame for any injury inflicted rests entirely with the intruder."

I personally never witnessed an attack by a tiger, but shortly after fieldwork began, Mel and Kirti had an encounter with Tigress Number One that neither will ever forget.

One morning Mel and his assistant, Sagar, found Number One and the Roaring Tigress together near the old Tractor Bridge and assumed they were feeding on a kill. Fifteen-foot-high grass and clumps of bushes bordered a small, meandering stream, and it was cool and damp beneath the dense vegetation, a perfect spot for a tigress to lie up with her kill. But there was no sound of flies; although Mel and Sagar searched, they could not find a carcass, but that was not unusual in such dense vegetation. They made a few notes, pinpointed the site on a map, and left. Next morning the Roaring Tigress was gone, but Number One was still there, and she was there again when they returned on the third day.

On the morning of the fourth day, nearly everyone in camp set out on elephants to try to capture more deer for Kirti's study. They approached several groups of deer without much luck; then, near the Dudora Stream, they finally managed to get close enough to dart a chital doe. They weighed, measured, and radio collared her, then waited nearby for her to recover from the drug. Afterward, since they were close to the Tractor Bridge, they decided to check whether Number One was still there.

Her radio signal was coming from the right place near the stream, but there was no sign of activity. Mel and Kirti moved the elephants in for a closer look. Progress was slow; small trees, thorn bushes, and ditches made maneuvering difficult; and the lead elephant carrying Kirti and Prem heaved and struggled against the wall of greenery. Both Mel and Kirti wore headphones and were trying to monitor the tigress's radio signal above the elephant's noise. They stopped to pinpoint Number One's position more exactly and found she was only a short distance away. Kirti climbed into a tree to get a better look into the grass. All three elephants were nervous, bunched close together, almost touching. Their stomachs rumbled and growled, and they slapped their trunks against the ground with loud, popping noises. Kirti was moving around in the tree, pointing with the long aluminum antenna. He began to speak; then everyone heard the miaow of a young cub.

Number One exploded out of the grass with a shattering roar. She made one leap up the tree and in a split second was on top of Kirti. He saw her coming and tried to ward her off with the antenna, but she flung it aside without noticing. She sank her claws into his thigh and buttocks and bit deeply into his leg. The force of her acceleration ripped Kirti off the branch and they both tumbled to the ground fifteen feet below.

No one could believe what was happening. Kirti's wife Pat repeated "Oh, my God," over and over again, her voice rising in hysteria, but everyone else was dumb with shock. Before anyone could move the tigress charged again, her roars blasting through the silence. The elephants spun on their heels and bolted in blind panic ahead of the enraged tigress. Nothing could stop them. Equipment flew everywhere in a wild confusion of screaming and trumpeting. People clung to ropes or whatever they could find, trying not to be swept off the elephants in the headlong dash through the bushes.

Seconds later Mel's elephant slammed to its knees; it had fallen into one of the hidden ditches. People pitched forward, then back as the elephant rose and lunged ahead, only to drop into another ditch a few yards further on. Mel flew over the elephant's head into the bushes, where he lay stunned while the elephant continued its escape. After about fifty yards Bodai, the driver, somehow managed to get the trembling beast under control and circled back. Mel, who was trying to stand, heard Sagar pleading with him to climb up, get back on the elephant because the tiger was coming, but he was dazed and unable to respond. Bodai finally managed to get the elephant to *cul*, or put her foot out to form a step, and Mel scrambled up the ten-foot wall of the animal's backside.

They reassembled the elephants a hundred yards from the tree. Pat was quiet, wide eyed, and everyone else was dazed. Regrouping, still in shock, everybody suddenly realized that they would have to go back in and face the tigress again. They had to find Kirti, whether he was alive or dead. The antennas were broken, and the other radio-tracking equipment was scattered all over the area. Now they had no way of knowing where the tigress was, and to get Kirti out meant that someone would have to be on the ground. The two project elephants refused to go back in. Bodai and Diplal, the drivers, whacked them fiercely with sticks, but the elephants only screamed and swung their heads from side to side, refusing to budge. Himal Kali, the government elephant, had taken part in many royal hunts and was not so easily frightened. Her driver eventually managed to coax her back toward the place where Kirti had fallen.

They found him deep in a tangle of grass and thorn bushes. When Number One had turned from him to attack the elephants, Kirti had managed to crawl a short distance toward the sound of voices. The grapefruit-sized wound on his thigh was bleeding very little, but his trousers were shredded and the claw marks in his buttocks looked deep and ragged. He had hurt his back in the fall from the tree and was in shock. Surprisingly, Himal Kali allowed herself to be persuaded to lie down, putting herself in an extremely vulnerable position, while Prem and the driver tried to get Kirti onto the pad. His back injury had left him unable to stand, but he could use his arms, so with his help they managed to hoist him onto the elephant's back.

No one was sure of the extent of Kirti's back injuries, and rather than risk the jolting elephant ride back to camp, they decided to take him to the Bhawanipur guardpost, half a mile away, and wait for the Jeep. Kirti was conscious, quite alert, but in a great deal of pain. The elephant drivers decided that Himal Kali was the fastest elephant, so with Mel on board they set out on the two-mile trip to camp. It was noon and the temperature was over a hundred degrees, but Himal Kali ran the whole way. She did not even pause to drink as they crossed the Rapti River but charged through the water like a tank, throwing up waves and spray.

Mel grabbed the first-aid kit, threw a mattress into the back of the Green Latrine, and prayed that today of all days it would start. It did, and he drove through the river and crossed without stalling, then bounced down the rutted bullock-cart track toward Bhawanipur. The ride in the Jeep would not be easy on Kirti's back, but it would be better than the same trip on the elephant. At the guardpost, people were pacing around nervously. Pat was worried that Kirti's back might be broken, and everyone knew a person with back injuries should be moved only with extreme care, but there was no choice. They loaded Kirti into the Green Latrine and inched slowly back to the river.

The road through the village of Sauraha was a joltingly uncomfortable cart track interrupted by small, unstable bridges, and there was yet another river crossing to navigate. At Tardi Bazaar, the junction with the main east-west highway, the surface improved and they were able to make better time. In less than an hour and a half they were approaching Bharatpur, the nearest town with any sort of medical facilities. On the way into town they drove past the small airstrip, where a Royal Nepal Airlines Twin Otter was taxiing to the end of the runway, ready to take off. It was the twice-weekly flight to Kathmandu, delayed because of bad weather. This chance encounter with the plane saved Kirti an agonizing drive over the Mahabharat Range to Kathmandu. The drive often took twelve hours in the best circumstances; with an injured person in the back it could have taken twice as long.

Six hours after the accident, Kirti was in Shanta Bawan Hospital in Kathmandu being treated by the best doctors in Nepal. He spent ten weeks fighting infection and received several skin grafts. His long and painful recovery took five months, but nine months after the accident he was back at work in Chitwan.

Kirti's mauling was the result of a mistake. "We should never have gone in there, and I should not have got off my elephant," he said later. He was lucky, for his injuries were relatively minor and he was not left permanently incapacitated, when he might easily have been killed. In 1985, a British ornithologist had not been so fortunate. He was leading a party of bird-watchers through Corbett National Park in northern India when he spotted an owl. Plunging into the jungle for a closer look, he literally stumbled upon a tigress with young cubs. She killed him and ate a portion of his leg. Later, other members of the bird-watching group agreed that the tigress was not at fault, for they had all seen very fresh tiger sign and were aware that the animal was nearby.

Tigers at their kills or tigresses with young cubs may occasionally attack if disturbed, but even when provoked they usually give people the opportunity to escape. If a tiger does kill someone under these circumstances, it does not automatically become a man-eater and in fact may never attack humans again. Neither is it always the case that the cubs of a man-eater will inherit this habit when they grow to adulthood.

A variety of experts have speculated on the reasons why tigers become man-eaters. Jim Corbett was of the opinion that "a man-eating tiger is a tiger that has been compelled, through stress of circumstances beyond its control, to adopt a diet that is alien to it. The stress of circumstances is, in nine cases out of ten, wounds and in the tenth, old age." He also believed that the changeover from animal to human flesh was, in most cases, accidental. As with most of Corbett's other observations on tiger behavior, these two explanations have stood the test of time, and most modern man-eaters fit into one or the other of Corbett's categories: they are wounded and unable to capture their natural prey, they are old and infirm, or they kill someone by accident. However, not even Corbett was able to offer any explanation of why some geographical areas are more prone to develop man-eaters than others.

There are no historical records of man-eaters in Chitwan, but 1979 saw the beginning of what has been termed an "outbreak" of man-killing that continues today. The only positive aspect of the Chitwan man-killings is that many of the tigers are animals with known life histories, invaluable information when it comes to piecing together the reasons why tigers become man-eaters. Most of the observations come from Chuck McDougal's long-term study of tigers around Tiger Tops and are a clear illustration of the value of such long-term studies.

The first incident happened in December of 1979 near Sauraha, not far from our camp. Early in the morning a young schoolteacher coming to the river for his daily bath climbed a small rise onto the riverbank and came face to face with a tiger that had approached the river from the other side. Another man walking about fifty yards behind the schoolteacher heard a scream and saw the victim struggling with the tiger. The tiger killed the teacher, then fled into a patch of nearby scrub. Fortunately the tiger was wearing a radio collar, so the researchers who were continuing the tiger study were able to locate and capture the animal and move it to the Kathmandu Zoo.

It was not difficult to sort out the circumstances that led this particular tiger to become a man-killer. He had been born to a tigress living near Tiger Tops, and when he was about two years old he left his mother's area and moved east toward Sauraha, where he got into a fight with another large male tiger. Prem and park warden Tirtha Maskey discovered him shortly after the fight; he was unable to move and had a seriously injured foreleg. They darted him, cleaned up his wounds, and attached a radio collar. He recovered from the injuries but was left with a permanent limp, and for the next year and a half the disabled tiger made his living along the edge of the park. His injured foreleg prevented him from catching wild prey, and he fed exclusively on cattle and domestic buffalo. It was almost inevitable that he would eventually maul or kill a person. Had he been left in the park after his attack on the schoolteacher, he might have gone on to become a habitual man-eater. He was a classic example of a tiger becoming a man-killer after being injured.

A different situation occurred in February of 1985, when a tigress began killing cattle and buffalo in Madi Valley, a finger of cultivated land that juts into the southern portion of Chitwan Park. One morning the villagers of Sitarpur found the tigress lying in a mustard field and stoned her. Instead of fleeing she moved further into the village and took refuge in a house. When the crowd gathered to stone her again, she mauled two men, then escaped and lay up in a small ravine near the village. After a few days, National Park authorities were able to dart her and took her to the park headquarters at Kasra. She was a very old animal, with badly worn canine teeth and several missing incisors. When she was killed a few days later, following a petition from the villagers, she was found to weigh only two hundred pounds, over a hundred pounds less than a healthy tigress.

Like the tiger that killed the schoolteacher, the Madi Tigress had never actually eaten a human, but she might have if she had been left in the park. Old and infirm, she was subsisting on domestic livestock, a diet that brought her into conflict with people. She clearly fit into Corbett's second category.

In 1984, a tiger that Chuck McDougal knew as Bange Bhale began to kill people; this tiger fit none of Corbett's categories. Bange Bhale was ousted from his territory by another male and subsequently became a transient, wandering well beyond his former range. In the space of a few months, he killed and ate three people. The fourth victim survived because he fended off Bange Bhale with a sickle, and shortly afterward Bange Bhale was captured and moved to the Kathmandu Zoo. He was eight to ten years old, in good health, and with no obvious injuries, a confirmed man-eater who did not fit any of the previous ideas of what a man-eater should be. Historically, there had always been a few of these oddball man-eaters, but people either assumed that Corbett was wrong and that man-eating was simply the nature of the beast, or that the wrong animal had been shot by mistake.

Today, with the wisdom of hindsight and the aid of Chuck McDougal's long-term monitoring, it seems we can now add another reason to the list of explanations of man-eating. Man-eating also involves tigers that have lost their home ranges to other tigers. This explanation may account for more man-eating than anyone had previously realized, because until recently there has been no background information on most man-eaters. Tigers ousted from their ranges tend to wander widely, get into fights with other tigers, and often end up in marginal areas where they live by killing domestic stock. This underlying social factor, fights with other tigers for territory, may even explain how tigers end up in Corbett's major category of "wounded and unable to hunt wild prey." Unfortunately, if this newly identified explanation is correct, then we can only expect man-eating to become more common over the next few decades.

Why is this? Recent efforts to save the tiger have effectively improved habitat conditions and increased the survivorship of animals living in protected areas. However, tigers are relatively long lived, and their social system limits the number of animals that can breed in a given area. Because females commonly maintain exclusive home ranges, and males likewise do not seem to share ranges with other males, there is a limit to the number of tigers of either sex that can be fitted into a given area such as Chitwan.

The problems begin when the number of young tigers looking for home ranges exceeds the number of home ranges that are vacant. If reserves are linked to other protected areas by corridors of forest, then the normal process of young animals leaving to search for a place to live can continue. But when protected areas are completely surrounded by agricultural land and villages, as many are, then both tigers and people are in trouble. With nowhere to go, young tigers may end up being forced to remain in the already "full" reserve. This overpopulation increases competition, especially among males, and we might expect more fights and more injuries. The only alternative for a young tiger born into a "full" reserve is to make a living along the margins of the reserve, feeding on cattle and domestic stock. Both of these options—increased male-male competition, and life quite literally on the edge—have the potential to produce man-eaters.

Ultimately, when all the reasons for tigers becoming man-eaters are finally understood, the answer to the question of why some geographical areas are more prone to the problem than others may be quite simple, perhaps as straightforward as the fact that some areas are better tiger habitat than others. High tiger densities may be part of the problem. Perhaps setting aside small, islandlike reserves of prime habitat where tigresses breed very successfully is a formula for producing man-eaters.

Unfortunately there are no simple and inexpensive solutions to the problem. It is easy to advocate larger and larger reserves, but it is usually impossible to implement such recommendations. Innovative short-term solutions like those currently being tried in the Indian Sunderbans may offer some help. There the authorities have started a unique experiment to protect the woodcutters and honey-gatherers who make their living in the forest. Lifelike human dummies are dressed in used clothing and fitted with electrical wires connected to a car battery. When touched, these dummies administer a nasty shock. The preliminary results suggest that tigers may be learning from this aversive therapy.

There is also the possibility that, given enough food, the tigers' social system does allow for some degree of "packing." Under certain circumstances, tigresses will allow their adult daughters to squeeze in beside them. However, there is a limit to how small an area each tigress can hold and still reproduce successfully. In the short term, habitat improvement schemes that prohibit cattle grazing, relocate villages, halt the annual burning of grassland and forest, and create more permanent water sources may be achieving this kind of packing. Although the immediate effect is to increase the tiger population, over the long term a larger number of tigers may well create a larger problem, one we were concerned to explore as the study continued.

Long-term solutions are more difficult, and whatever measures are tried will probably have to be tailored to the needs of particular areas. In general, buffer zones will be essential, especially where it proves impossible to link tiger populations by corridors between reserves and forests. Chuck McDougal's long-term study of tigers in Chitwan has proved its usefulness in the case of man-killers, and similar studies in other problem areas might go a long way toward identifying the full range of circumstances that produce man-eaters.

6   Grass Cutters

*T*RAVELING THROUGH THE TALL grasslands of Chitwan is a slow business. Even riding on an elephant, the feathery seed heads and thick, serrated leaves reach far above your head. You can see nothing except a wall of trembling grass and the sky. The sheer mass of vegetation is overwhelming, and the noise of the elephant struggling through seas of tangled blades is almost deafening. Thick, bamboolike canes whip your face, while fluffy grass seeds and other debris rain down from above. Periodically the elephant is slowed, then stopped by an impenetrable clump. At a command from the driver, it whacks the offending mass of grasses with its trunk, swinging its head from side to side in a gigantic effort to part the house-high hay field. To move through these grasses successfully, you need to be either a very large, powerful, shoving machine like the elephant and rhino, or small and nimble like the scuttling hog deer.

There are paths and tunnels beneath this giant lush lawn that are large enough for a man to walk through. Made by rhinos and marked with dung, the tunnels twist and turn so you can never see more than a few feet ahead. Should you meet a rhino, there is no place to go except back; the walls of grass on either side are as impenetrable as a woven bamboo mat.

Once a year most of the grass burns to the ground, leaving only a few charred canes. Suddenly, you can see—the maze of trails becomes a network of beaten paths among the burned stubble. It looks desolate and beyond repair. Bleached skulls and the mouse-nibbled bones of old tiger kills shine white against the black earth, and sooty rhinos wander through the ruined landscape chewing on scorched grass canes.

It seems incredible that such a mass of vegetation can suddenly disappear—millions of tons vaporized, turned to ashes and smoke overnight. But historically, fire has played a major role in shaping these grasslands, and grass is a remarkably persistent plant. Unlike the leaves of trees and shrubs, grasses have a continuously active growing point at the base of the leaf. Instead of branching, the veins of grass leaves run in straight, parallel lines directly from base to tip. The growing point is shielded from fire and grazing animals, and even if the entire leaf is removed the plant can rapidly grow back to its original height. This ability to rapidly replace grazed or burned leaves, coupled with the fact that a large proportion of the growth is edible, have made grasslands one of the most productive ecosystems on earth. A square mile of grassland is capable of supporting a greater biomass of mammals, birds, and insects than any other kind of terrestrial habitat.

A variety of mammals in Chitwan include grass in their diet. Rhino are the major consumers, followed by hog deer, chital, and sambar. Gaur come down from the hills in spring to feed on new shoots after the fires, and wild boar eat grass as well as fruits and tubers. A hundred years ago there were three other large mammalian grass eaters in Chitwan: barasingha, wild water buffalo, and elephant. No one knows how abundant they were or what effect their combined presence had on the grasses, but they are now gone from Chitwan and all three are endangered species, as are hog deer and rhino.

From studies in Africa, we do know that the grazing of ungulates can influence the structure of grasslands and the quality of grass they produce. Different species of grazing mammals feed on different parts of the grass. In general, nonruminants like rhinos and elephants can survive on older, coarser grass than ruminants like deer. The feeding of the larger grazers opens up clumps of tall grass and stimulates new shoot production; the smaller, more selective feeders can then get at the grass and herbs closer to the ground.

Obviously, the grasslands of the Serengeti and those of the *terai* differ enormously in rainfall patterns, grass production, and complement of grazing animals. With the possible exception of elephants, none of the *terai* grazers make long seasonal migrations. Sambar, chital, and hog deer spend their lives in very small areas, and even rhino have small ranges. However, as in the Serengeti, the larger *terai* grazers such as rhino, buffalo, and elephant, which feed on coarse, low-protein growth probably facilitate the feeding of smaller, more selective herbivores such as deer. No one has calculated what effect the local extinctions of major grazing species have had on the structure and species composition of the *terai* grasslands, but the effect could well be considerable.

Like the large mammalian grazers, people have been cutting and cropping these grasslands for centuries. Since at least the eighteenth century, grasslands have been burned regularly to provide grazing for thousands of cattle and buffalo in the dry season. The primitive Tharu people who have lived for generations in the *terai* regularly harvest the grasses and use them for almost every conceivable construction purpose. Only the corner posts and main roof beams of their houses are made of wood; everything else is grass and mud. They use some short grasses for thatching roofs and other species for rope. The tall, bamboolike canes of the "elephant" grasses are woven together with yet another type of grass to form the house walls. The grass walls are then covered with a mixture of mud and cow dung that dries to a smooth, clean, plasterlike finish. Grasses are also used to make a variety of other items including fences, flares, fishtraps, and scarecrows.

Until thirty years ago the grasses were readily available near every village, but the large-scale resettlement of hill people into the *terai* quickly transformed the region into farmland. Grasslands were the first to go: they were flat and simple to clear, and the soil was fertile and easily tilled with a bullock-drawn plow. In less than twenty years all that remained of the once-extensive natural grasslands was enclosed within a few reserves and national parks. The people had plowed up the source of their major construction material.

Inevitably, the reserves have become a focus of resentment for the local people. Inside the boundary, they see miles of untouched grass. Not only are they prevented from harvesting their traditional source of building material, but the reserves harbor all manner of wildlife that move into the fields at night to feed on their crops. Heavy monsoon rains and flooding wash away fences and ditches, and the National Parks and Wildlife Department authorities admit they do not have the resources to build or maintain better barriers.

Someone once asked the obvious question: Why not encourage each family to grow its own supply of grass for house construction? This seems like a simple solution until you realize how little land each family has and how intensively they farm every tiny piece. On average, an acre of land supports a family of six people. Most families grow three crops a year. Rice is planted at the beginning of the monsoon and harvested between November and December. Wheat and mustard are the major winter crops, while maize, barley, millet, chilis, and tobacco are also grown. In the few weeks between harvesting and replanting, village cattle are turned out into the stubble to graze, and their dung provides the fertilizer for the next crop.

Once the main support beams of a Tharu house are in place, construction relies entirely on grasses and then adobe.

The situation is fraught with difficulty for the authorities in charge, and the Wildlife Department has been forced to experiment with a practical, low-budget method of maintaining the peace between humans and wildlife. They have chosen to compensate the farmers for their crop losses in building materials rather than cash: once a year, for fifteen days, people are allowed into the parks and reserves to harvest grass. A permit system is imposed as a way of keeping track of numbers; each permit costs two cents and admits one family. Fees are intentionally kept to a minimum to encourage everyone to register, so the sale of permits raises little revenue for the National Parks Department; the total amount raised annually is less than a thousand dollars. The real money is generated by the sale of grass. Nearly a half-million dollars' worth of grass products are bought, sold, and traded each year, with a significant impact on the local economy.

Heavily grazed pasture and fields outside the park were once tall grasslands.

Villagers gathering to buy grass-cutting permits.

The harvest season begins in January, and days before the official opening, people within a fifty-mile radius start to converge on the park. Crowds of men, women, and children camp near the official check-posts; some bring bullock carts to carry away the grass, others carry the grass they harvest to nearby villages on their own backs. Still others will hire out their labor to entrepreneurs who ship the grass further away and sell it far from the park. Most people come with their families to harvest enough grass to repair their old houses or build new ones. To prevent overexploitation, no vehicles of any kind are allowed into the park, and people are permitted to take out only what they can carry on their backs. Even with this restriction, between fifty and one hundred thousand tons of grass are taken from the park each year.

For us, the grass-cutting season was a strange and busy interlude in our research routine. As a rule, we rarely saw anyone on our daily tiger-tracking rounds, but for fifteen days in January the grasslands were invaded by a hundred thousand people. The first day of the season was bedlam, as thousands of people crowded around the tiny warden's office in the foggy dawn, jostling to buy permits. Early arrivals had the advantage in that they could stake out the closest and best areas of grass for their families. Minor fights and shoving matches broke out, and the park warden alternately shouted and pleaded for order as he was overwhelmed by the pushing crowd.

Once families acquired their cutting permits they hurried down to the river crossing, where lines of excited, shouting men and women filed into the waist-deep water. For hours, thousands of them crossed the river and disappeared into the foggy grasslands. During the day while we searched for tigers, the sounds of singing and shouting echoed from every meadow. The villagers called back and forth to one another as they worked and posted small boys in trees to act as lookouts for rhinos and sloth bears. The people knew we were searching for tigers and viewed our approach with apprehension, as if by merely coming near them we might attract a tiger. However, most of the tigers moved away from the noise of people and took refuge in the forested parts of their ranges during the grass-cutting season.

At dusk, roads and trails were congested with knots of people carrying bundles of grass. They looked like trotting haystacks, bur-

Grass cutters wade the Rapti River.

dened down as they were with fifty or sixty pounds of grass. Insulated from the jungle sounds by their loads, the people traveled in nervous groups, and a start of panic from one person would send the rest of the party into the bushes. Everyone had to be out of the park by sunset, so the rush was on to make the river crossing while it was still light. Some waded with their loads, and others balanced the bundles precariously on narrow dugout canoes that floated gingerly across with only an inch of freeboard.

Carrying grass across the Rapti River.

Villagers carry enormous bundles of grass out of the park.

Every evening the warden was kept busy with rumors of people being killed or mauled by tigers. The tales grew in the telling and spread like wildfire through the camped grass cutters. One evening there was a report of a woman bleeding to death after an encounter with a tiger. It sounded serious, so Prem, Mel, and the warden spent all the next day checking with everyone who had heard the story. They finally managed to track the woman down, and she emerged from her house with a bloodstained cloth wrapped around her arm. It turned out that she had cut herself with a sickle while cutting grass.

Villagers spent the first week harvesting the waist-high thatch grasses; then they set fires in the areas of tall grass. The dry outer leaves burned like tinder, flames burst out of dense grass thickets, and the snapping, crackling sounds of fires erupted from all corners of the floodplain. Columns of thick smoke and the roar of burning filled the air, while clouds of drongos and rollers perched on the edges of the inferno, swooping down to pick off insects flushed out by the flames. In the evenings the air was still and hot, heavy with smoke. The fires eventually spread to the forested Siwalik hills, and at night the lines of flames inching round the distant hills looked like fiery dragons tonguing the sky.

Although it seems that nothing could escape the flames, not everything burns. Fires are patchy, even in the grasslands, and most of them are extinguished at night by the heavy fog. Tall, damp reeds around the rivers and *tals* are too wet to burn, and in other places winds cause the flames to skip large patches of ground. Because many of the grassland areas are burned every year or two, there is little accumulation of dead leaves, and lack of fuel causes the fires to move quickly and burn at relatively cool temperatures. The flames strip away the outer silica-laden leaves of the tall grasses, leaving the thick stalks intact. The canes are more difficult to harvest and command a higher price in the market, because when they are woven into mats with grass rope they are used as the base for both interior and exterior walls in

*Village woman
cutting tall grasses.*

Bundles of grass on the riverbank will be carted to nearby villages.

almost every house in the region. Although the canes are much in demand, the harvest barely makes a dent in the supply.

Toward the end of the fifteen-day grass-cutting season, we saw fewer and fewer people. Most of the activity became concentrated along the riverbanks, where grass bundles were stacked like sheaves of wheat after a harvest. Bullock-cart drivers haggled with villagers over the cost of transporting grass to the nearest town, and the roads were clogged with slow lines of loaded carts. It took the heavily laden carts almost all day to travel the five miles to Tardi Bazaar.

After two weeks of intense activity, the park reverted to its normal, quiet rhythms. A glimmer of green touched the meadows, and the scarlet flowers of the silk cotton trees began to fall, scattering on the blackened ground. In the late afternoons and evenings, groups of chital and hog deer emerged to feed on the new grass and fat red flowers. This is the only time of year when hog deer are found in large herds, and chital form aggregations of a hundred or more in the open meadows. There is not enough cover for tigers to hunt these large herds successfully, and most of the kills are made along the edges of the now open grasslands or in unburned grasses along streams and wet areas. Within a month the grasses are knee-high, the deer herds fragment and scatter, there is enough stalking cover for tigers, and we began to find their kills in the grasslands again.

For the fifty thousand or so people who live near the park, it and its regulations are a continual source of irritation, loss of livelihood, and on some occasions, even loss of life. Considered from the villagers' point of view, the park is essentially a liability: they derive almost no benefits from it but have to live with the numerous constraints it imposes on their lives.

Ram Bahadur and his family live at the edge of the park in the small village of Jaimangala. Just a few yards from their house, a ditch and sagging barbed-wire fence mark the beginning of the protected area, out of bounds to his family and livestock. Before the area was made into a park, Ram used to graze his cattle and buffalo there, but now one of his sons must take the livestock several miles each day to find grazing. The family also used to collect wood for their cooking fire in the forest, but now one of the family must walk five to ten miles daily to find enough wood to cook the evening meal of rice.

The demand for firewood is reducing Nepal's forests at a dangerous rate.

If Ram's cattle wander into the park, they will be rounded up by the park guards and taken to the local pound; Ram will have to pay a fine of five rupees (forty cents) per head to reclaim them. Once the family's prized milch buffalo escaped through a gap in the fence and wandered away into the park's lush grassland. The family searched for her all day, but when they finally found her, the valuable animal was dead, killed by a tiger. Because it is illegal to allow domestic animals into the park, Ram could not claim compensation; indeed, he could have been fined.

Ram's biggest complaint about the park concerns the wildlife. At night, wild boar, rhino, and deer leave the park and invade his small fields. The highly endangered rhinos are the worst offenders, for their great feet flatten the crops and crush at least as much as they eat. It is all but impossible to protect the ripening grain from the rhinos' nightly forays, especially on moonless or misty nights. According to Ram, the best way to minimize crop damage is for one person to spend the night on a platform, or *machan*, on stilts in each field. The watcher must stay awake and alert all night, listening and looking. When he hears or sees something, he shouts and bangs a tin kettle to frighten the animal and arouse nearby crop watchers ensconced on similar *machans* nearby. The drawbacks of this crop protection scheme are that the *machans* are cold and uncomfortable, and if the watcher is doing his job, he gets no sleep. Ram says that after a night in the *machan*, he is too tired to do his normal day's work, and the family's income suffers as a result.

In 1977 and 1978, John Milton and George Binney conducted a survey of villagers and their attitudes toward the National Park. They found that despite makeshift fences, flares, and crop watchers, almost every farming household in Jaimangala reported staggering annual crop losses due to wildlife damage. In Jaimangala, villagers estimated that they lost eighty-five percent of their rice, eighty percent of their wheat, and ninety percent of their maize crops to animals. The greater the distance between fields and the park boundary, the smaller the losses.

When asked what the government should do to protect their crops, most people suggested a high concrete wall to keep the rhinos out of their fields. The majority of people surveyed in Jaimangala suggested that the government should move the entire village to an unspecified place nearby where there were no rhinos but where there were comparably fertile soils, water, and a forest where they could graze their animals and cut firewood.

Since there was an alternative area available, the government took on the mammoth task of resettling some of the most seriously

affected villages. However, there were limited funds and, more important, not very many areas of suitable farmland that could accommodate an entire village. Only ten of the three hundred and twenty villages
that surround the park could be moved. No matter how large or small a
park is, farmland and park boundaries will always border each other,
and crop raiding by wildlife will always be a problem.

Even in Western countries, reserves and national parks provoke
major conflicts with the surrounding populations. In Europe the problem may be as simple as traffic jams caused by day visitors and pick-
nickers. In the northeastern United States, deer and other wildlife may
be a source of irritation as they feed in carefully tended vegetable gar-
dens. The primary difference is that in less-developed countries the
conflicts tend to be more intense, because at issue frequently are not
irritations but losses that affect the basic survival of the surrounding
human population.

In Chitwan, Hemanta Mishra and the park authorities have identified four major areas of conflict and are attempting to walk the tight-
rope of regulation and common sense, balancing the needs of the
people against the survival of the park and its wildlife. On the positive
side, the park does bring a few small benefits to the local population.
There are limited seasonal employment opportunities with the park
service and some of the tourist hotels, but in general most of the positions go to better-educated Nepalis from Kathmandu. Tourism really
has not brought as much money into the local economy as was originally promised. In fact, tourism has left most of the poorer villagers
worse off than before, because prices of basic commodities like rice,
vegetables, cooking oil, and kerosene have increased much more rapidly in areas where tourists concentrate. A few traders and merchants
from nearby towns are doing well, but most of the villagers lose.

The major benefit of the national park is soil and water conservation, the advantages of which are vividly demonstrated along the riverbanks. Most of the park is bounded by rivers, and the contrast between
the overgrazed, eroded bank outside the park and the more stable bank
inside the park is a graphic illustration of the values of maintaining
vegetative cover. Unfortunately, even with this classic example of the
benefits of soil conservation right before them, most of the villagers
regard erosion and floods as acts of God rather than mismanagement.
Soil and water conservation in regional terms is simply too great an
abstraction; the villagers' most pressing concern is the crop in the field
at the moment and the next meal for their families.

Since 1977, the park authorities have tried to increase communication between park staff and local residents. A group of villagers,

schoolteachers, and local leaders meets annually for two days to discuss the problems and needs of the park and its surrounding population. The meetings give people a chance to air their grievances and blow off steam. They also give park staff an opportunity to explain the complexities of management problems to the people. The major impact of the meetings has been to bring the two sides together and let the villagers become involved in decisions that affect their daily lives.

The grass harvest has also been a major public relations tool. By allowing people limited access to a resource that is central to their lives, the program illustrates a principle of conservation in terms that the villagers can understand. They may not know or care about ecosystem conservation and endangered species, but they do recognize that most of the tall grasses outside the park have disappeared and that the reserve is protecting those that remain in the district.

From the park authorities' point of view, the grass harvest is valuable as an educational and public relations tool as well as a management technique. Grasslands are a successful stage, highly productive in terms of wildlife and crucial for the preservation of the endangered rhino, hog deer, and tiger. The *terai* grasslands are maintained by a combination of fire, grazing, flooding, and human activity, and the grass-cutting program may be an economical way of maintaining the ecosystem.

The situation in the *terai* is extremely unusual in that the authorities are dealing with a very rapidly renewing resource. Fuel wood, timber, or rhinos could not be exploited in the same manner by the same numbers of people. In the long term, the demand for grass will probably outstrip the supply, and the system of harvesting will have to be altered, but for the moment it is a practical trade-off and an effective means of compensating villagers, at least in part, for their crop losses.

It is difficult to estimate the effects of this annual short-term but massive influx of people on the park. We found that tigers and deer simply moved away from the disturbance, but we had no way of knowing how small mammals, reptiles, and birds were affected by the fires. Although vegetational changes over the past ten years have not been measured, villagers believe the taller "elephant grass" is spreading at the expense of the short thatching grass. No one knows if this is a normal part of the dynamics of these alluvial grasslands or if it is a response to cutting and burning, but a study of the fire and range ecology of grasslands in Chitwan is now underway.

7 Views from a Hide

$\mathcal{W}$E PEERED AT THE flimsy blind through the dim dawn light. Bodai, the elephant driver, clicked his tongue disapprovingly. "No good," he said. "You can't stay there. It's too dangerous." Bodai nudged the elephant closer. My prospective hiding place was three feet square and consisted of four tree branches stuck into the mud. A few feet off the ground they drooped over to form a roof of sorts, but the sides were thin and almost leafless in places. We could see straight through it.

When I didn't go with Mel to radio track animals, I spent a great deal of time crouched in small blinds or hides, photographing the wildlife in Chitwan. It was rewarding work. Besides providing documentation of what animals were around, there were wonderful opportunities to view unsuspecting birds and mammals as they went about their daily activities. Some hides were temporary, set up only for photographing specific animals or a certain kind of behavior. Others were more permanent, and I used them regularly for taking photos of a variety of animals. I could easily walk to some hides from our camp, but it was best to travel by elephant to those further away. Elephant back was not only safer from rhinos but made carrying cameras, lens, film, a tripod, and other paraphernalia much easier.

This flimsy blind Bodai and I were looking at was my mistake. The day before, I had seen a great deal of activity around this particular rhino wallow on Itarni Island. Full of enthusiasm for the photos I might be able to take, I had asked one of the *shikaris* to help me build a blind. Later, diverted by other tasks, I had been forced to describe what I wanted, and where, but my command of Nepali obviously had been inadequate. Now we saw the result. I wondered what to do. If I returned to camp, I would have wasted not only my morning but also the time of an elephant and driver. The alternative was to try and make a few quick improvements and hope for the best.

Fiona making some adjustments to a permanent hide.

Bodai cut more branches, and I threaded them into the existing framework until it was slightly less transparent. As I listened to the noise of the elephant leaving and wondered if my decision to stay had been wise, it was too late for second thoughts.

The blind was set in a small grassy glade, the centerpiece of which was a dark, milk tea–colored wallow that smelled strongly of rhino urine. Swollen by recent rain, the waters reached to within ten yards of my hiding place. I set up the camera, organized my belongings, and began the silent wait, ears pricked for advance warning of activity. Birds captured my attention to begin with. Red-vented bulbuls splashed and fluffed their feathers in the evil-smelling water. Two matronly peahens, handsome in their autumn-leaf finery, sailed majestically out of the shadows to sip their morning drink, and somewhere in the branches above, a brown fish owl chuckled like an old man.

Sitting in a blind is not nearly as boring as it sounds. In some ways it is like being out in the forest at night. Vision is restricted and you have to locate and identify sounds, categorize them before their source comes into sight: birds hopping; the slow, nervous steps of a barking deer; wild piglets screaming at their mother for milk. Some creatures like jungle fowl make far too much noise for their size, and others like the giant sambar deer are there before you know it and, just as silently, are gone.

I watched a wasp stuffing paralyzed spiders into the end of a broken grass cane. It hunted close by, two feet above the round, flying silent sorties in search of prey, then stooping like a tiny hawk. One by one it brought the spiders back to the quarter-inch hole, staggering in the air under their weight. After the eleventh spider, the hole was full. The wasp patted the pile with its antennas for a long time before it seemed satisfied, then arched its abdomen and laid a single translucent egg on the crowd of feebly waving legs. She flew off and returned with a load of mud, sealed the nest, then left and did not return. The wasp had done all she could to ensure the growth and survival of her offspring and was probably searching for more holes and more spiders to fill them.

Like a clockwork toy, a pinkish-brown, bristly mongoose alternately ran and stopped to listen its way across the glade in front of me. It rooted fiercely in a pile of leaves, back arched, pouncing and chewing on invisible morsels. As I focused the camera and took a single picture, it leaped in the air, gave my mound of branches a suspicious stare, and left. Simultaneously, a heavy crashing sound made me jump just like the nervous mongoose. Only a rhino would make such a racket. "Oh God, I hope it doesn't walk right over me," I thought, and crouched behind my feeble shelter of leaves and twigs.

Although most rhinos are not nasty tempered, my fear of meeting them at close quarters bordered on paranoia. Having watched them push their way through thickets of thorns and vines that would have stopped an elephant, I had come to the conclusion that no hiding place on the ground was safe from their powerful bodies.

Because Andrew Laurie had been studying the rhinos in Chitwan, he knew their personalities and quirks. He could anticipate which rhinos might be provoked by a small sound or smell and charge for no apparent reason, and which would run away from the noise of a branch breaking. Andrew learned that male rhinos fight each other frequently and often fatally; nearly one third of all rhino deaths, excluding those related to poaching, resulted from wounds inflicted during fights. Dominant males and females with calves were the most aggressive, while young adults usually fled from people and strange noises. We too learned to recognize a few individuals like Mr. Plod, who spent his time near our camp, and Stumptail, who was fierce and seemed to fight a lot, but we were never at ease with them as Andrew was.

Rhinos kill and injure many more people a year in Chitwan than do tigers or leopards. Rhinos have unexpectedly large, sharp teeth, which they use as weapons when fighting with one another. You may think of being trampled or perhaps gored by a rhino, but it is their sharp, slashing teeth that usually do the most damage. For some unaccountable reason, most of the tourists visiting Chitwan are relatively unafraid of rhinos. Accompanied by a village boy with a stick as a hired guide, parties of them chatter casually along trails surrounded by ten-foot-high elephant grass. One reads about terrified tourists marveling at brave biologists, but in this case the positions were reversed.

Purney is a cheerful, gregarious man employed by the national park as a driver. One morning he was traveling slowly down the main park road on a tractor when he thought he heard a voice calling to him. He stopped the vehicle and listened, but there was no sound, so he decided he had imagined the call and continued on his way. On the way back, he heard the voice again in the same place, so he went to investigate. Twenty yards from the road, he found a man lying beneath a tree. As Purney approached, the man opened his arms to display a huge slice in his abdomen and his intestines covered with grass and earth. "What happened?" Purney asked in horror.

Calmly, the man related his story. He was a tailor who lived in a nearby village and regularly traveled through the park to the market in Bharatpur to buy cloth. He often saw and heard rhinos but had managed to scare them off by shouting or had climbed a tree until they went away. Early that morning he had been walking quietly down the road when he heard a rhino. He stopped to listen and suddenly, without warning, the rhino charged. It was a female with a half-grown calf. He leaped for a nearby tree, grasped a branch with his arms, pulled his feet up, and hung six feet off the ground. The rhino rushed by with raised head and hit him, knocking him to the ground with the force of its charge. It came back and rolled him over, slashing with its powerfully sharp teeth, cutting open his belly and trampling him. Then it left.

The man had lain there for a long time, hoping that someone would come along. He had bought a sari for his wife, some pieces of cloth, and gifts for his two small children. Of the hundred rupees he had taken shopping, he still had fifty left, and he offered the money to Purney if he would take the things to his wife and tell her what had

LEADER:WILMA HARLEY
FOR DATE:01/23/99 (CND)

ARRIVE 1000   DEPART 100

MEMO : CK#198805 $417.00
PURCHASE DATE 01/08/99

TOT.CHGS: $1,667.50
DEPOSIT: $417.00
CODE: Group

PACK 360

13	LUNCH	:	No Avail
13	OMNI	: 1:00 PM	: Places
13	MUSEUM	:	: Museum

ACCT #: 630931   G   G   (CND)   GRADE: NR to NR
ARRIVE 930   DEPART 330   MEMO : VISA $29.00 THANK YOU
NOTE: PURCHASE DATE 01/08/99

TOT.CHGS: $117.00
DEPOSIT: $29.00
CODE: Group

---

(717)796-3441
LEADER:BRIAN SANTELL
FOR DATE:01/23/99 (MER)

78	LUNCH	:	:No Need
78	PLANET	:11:15 AM	: Starry
78	OMNI	: 1:00 PM	: Places
78	MUSEUM	:	: Museum

ACCT #: 630033   G   G   (KLC)   GRADE: NR to NR
ARRIVE 945   DEPART 400   MEMO : CK#1027 $205.00
NOTE: SEE F6 MEMO   PURCHASE DATE 01/19/99

TOT.CHGS: $819.00
DEPOSIT: $205.00
CODE: Group

PACK # 93

---

(717)569-9767
LEADER:TIM EFINGER
FOR DATE:01/23/99 (JAD)

53	LUNCH	:	:NoBuying
53	PLANET	: 2:15 PM	: Starry
53	OMNI	:12:00 PM	: Places
53	MUSEUM	:	: Museum

ACCT #: 519293   U   G   (SUN)   GRADE: NR to NR
ARRIVE N/A   DEPART 200   MEMO : 25%DEPOSIT/VISA $244.00
NOTE: PURCHASE DATE 01/15/99

TOT.CHGS: $488.50
DEPOSIT: $244.00
CODE: Group

TEMPLE UNIVERSITY UPWARD BOUND

---

(215)204-5132
LEADER:NAMIDRAH BYRD
FOR DATE:01/23/99 (SUN)

INTERIM HOUSE WEST

SEATS	SPACE		TIME	EVENT	GRADE
50	LUNCH	:	12:45 PM	: Name-A	
50	PLANET	:	2:15 PM	: Starry	
50	OMNI	:	11:00 AM	: Place	
50	MUSEUM	:		: Museum	

ACCT #: 577011   (JAD)   GRADE: NR to NR
ARRIVE 1000   DEPART 330   MEMO : CK#1092 $552.00
NOTE: PURCHASE DATE 01/08/99

(215)871-0300   (215)871-0300
LEADER:DONNA WILLIAMS
FOR DATE:01/23/99 (MBR)

TOT CHGS: $250.00
DEPOSIT: $552.00
CODE: Soc Serv

MENTORS FOR BERKS YOUTH PROGRAM

48	MUSEUM	:		: Museum	*MIXED
48	OMNI	:	11:00 AM	: Places	*MIXED
48	LUNCH	:		: No Need	*MIXED

ACCT #: 603199   (KLC)   GRADE : NR to NR
ARRIVE 100   DEPART 500   MEMO : CK#182 $101.00
NOTE: PURCHASE DATE 12/14/98

(610)607-6261
LEADER:CHRISTINE MARINO
FOR DATE:01/23/99 (KWK)

TOT CHGS: $404.00
DEPOSIT: $101.00
CODE: Group

MERCER COUNTY COMMUNITY COLLEGE PROJECT SMILE

175	LUNCH	:		: No Need	*MIXED
175	PLANET	:	12:15 PM	: Starry	*MIXED
175	OMNI	:	11:00 AM	: Places	*MIXED
175	MUSEUM	:			

happened. He asked for a drink of water. Purney ran to a nearby stream and carried water back in his hat. Then he ran to find help, but by the time Purney and the rescuers reached him, the man was dead.

Purney had told us his story only recently, and the scene replayed itself in my mind as I listened to the heavy, shuffling steps approach the wallow. A round gray shape appeared at the edge of the trees. The rhino peered around myopically, ears flapping. Its caution and relatively smooth skin gave me hope; this must be a young animal, I thought, unsure of itself and probably not dangerous to people. After considerable snuffling and peering, the rhino walked down to the wallow and settled into the water with a loud sigh.

An hour of quiet wallowing interspersed with occasional earflicks and bubbles of gas gave me confidence. I took a few pictures and smiled at the frogs struggling to maintain a foothold on the rhino's shifting bulk. The forest was quieter now, the sun was well above the horizon, and almost everything had retreated into the green shade of the trees. My hiding place became hotter and hotter. Sweat gathered on my forehead and dripped into my eyes. I tied a handkerchief around my head, but soon that too began to drip. The camera was almost too hot to handle, its blackness having soaked up the sun's heat even faster than I. I wondered if the film inside would cook; maybe none of this was worthwhile.

Suddenly I could hear the "Phuh-phuh-phuh" of distant rhinos, fighting or courting. The sound came closer and turned into a squeaking bray, like an oversized, irate donkey, and I knew the rhinos were mating. Andrew called the noise a "squeak-pant," and it meant a male was chasing a female. Then, with a noise like a train, they burst into the clearing—not two rhinos, but three. All of them, to my untutored eye, seemed to be highly enraged. The smooth, wallowing rhino stood up with a snort of alarm and backed off into the bushes. The largest of the three intruders gazed round truculently, then lifted his tail and jetted a pulsing stream of urine ten feet behind him as he walked slowly toward the water. With rising panic, I recognized his deeply grooved horn and scarred rump. It was Triscar, a bad-tempered male who was unafraid of elephants and who had already killed two people.

Triscar settled into the water with a grunt while the other three rhinos and I watched to see what he would do next. After a few minutes, the smooth rhino made a move toward the wallow, causing Triscar to half rise to his feet in disapproval. While Triscar wallowed, the three other rhinos spread out and began to graze quietly in the clearing. I was surrounded.

The smooth, young rhino.

There were no nearby trees I could climb, and it would be difficult to sneak away unnoticed. Staying put was the only option. For an hour I watched them. The smooth rhino managed to edge his way back into the wallow and settled down to sleep. Triscar flapped his ears but did not move. One of the other rhinos wandered off into the forest, while the female continued to graze. I realized I was missing the opportunity for some good close-up pictures. The first time the shutter clicked, Triscar raised his head. I tried again. Triscar exploded out of the wallow in a flurry of smelly mud and water, charging straight at the smooth rhino, who rapidly retreated.

I watched through the camera as Triscar swung his head in my direction, squinted peevishly at my hiding place, and started toward me, sniffing like a hound. I stared in horror as his bulk filled, then overflowed the viewfinder. He was six feet away, then two, and finally his nose touched the branches. All I could hear was the sound of his breath. I felt as if I had suddenly been drained of all strength; I was incapable of movement, aware only of his breathing and the thunderous sound of blood rushing round inside my head. "He's going to catch my scent and kill me," I thought.

He opened his mouth, exposing two long, sharp teeth that lay almost flat against his lower jaw. "Just like enormous pig tusks," I thought irrelevantly, as he took a mouthful of leaves from my shelter. I could have reached out and touched his huge lips without straightening my arm. He munched and snuffled, while I leaned back as far as I could. I had visions of the hide being eaten away, slowly exposing me to his view, but there was nothing I could do. I closed my eyes and clamped my teeth together to stop them from chattering.

After he had eaten half of one side of the hide he walked into some nearby bushes and stayed there for the next forty minutes while I trembled, certain that he would pick up my scent now he had moved downwind. I was lucky; he was more concerned with feeding.

At noon Bodai and the elephant returned to pick me up. Bodai was taken aback by my incoherent cries of joy but tut-tutted when he saw the large footprints next to the hide. Out by the river we met Triscar again, grazing stolidly in the tall reeds. He snorted and charged the elephant, but she trumpeted loudly and popped her trunk against the ground, warning him that she was not intimidated by his threats. He stopped, raised his head and sniffed, then lumbered off and began grazing again.

When I told Mel about my encounter with Triscar, he was furious. He reminded me of how critical we had been of other people's careless behavior around rhinos and how lucky I'd been to escape unharmed,

This pied kingfisher is one of four kingfisher species commonly seen along the rivers.

particularly because the rhino was Triscar. As it turned out, I had done the right thing by pure chance. If I had tried to run and climb a tree Triscar almost certainly would have caught me.

Very little of my time in hides was so dramatic. Often I spent a whole day inadvertently watching people as they fished or grazed their livestock; I usually kept quiet and waited, hoping they would move on. Once three village women with hand-woven fishing nets and cane baskets tied to their hips worked their way along the riverbank toward me. Waist deep in the water, they scooped armfuls of weed out onto the bank and sorted through it for fish. A few feet in front of my blind, they realized someone was watching them. "Who's there?" they asked, embarrassed and giggling. When I emerged, they seemed relieved that I was a woman and could speak a little Nepali, but they were astonished that anyone would sit in a tiny grass hut in the middle of nowhere. "What are you doing?" the oldest one queried. "Waiting for the ducks to come closer so I can photograph them," I replied weakly, aware of how eccentric the answer must sound to someone who spends sixteen hours a day cooking, washing, and working in the fields. They glanced at each other and then at the river, where of course there were no ducks in sight.

For the next half hour I helped the women sort through piles of weeds and enlarged my limited knowledge of river fish in Chitwan. A minnow-sized, silvery-white species that puffs up like a Ping-Pong ball when touched was no good to eat. The best way to kill a thrashing, four-foot eel is to bite it quickly just behind the head; eels make excellent curry. Tiny, transparent river shrimp are valuable—they fetch a good price in the local market.

The period of quiet after the women went on their way was surprisingly brief, as though the birds had been waiting for the disturbance to pass. Within a few minutes, a strutting crow pheasant appeared to peck through the debris left by the fishing women, and a pied kingfisher perched on a log a few feet away. The lowering copper-gold sun laid a long, glistening path on the water, transforming the wading birds into slim silhouettes, while early evening swallows and pratincoles wheeled and twittered like bats.

The time before dusk is filled with suspense and anticipation. It is the time when most of the night animals start to move, and for a photographer it is a race against the fading light. A movement in the tall grass caught my eye and I stared at the spot for a long time, seeing only a faint, sporadic quivering of grass stems. The shadowed stems dissolved into a pattern of dots and circles—a leopard, no, three leopards, half-grown cubs, playing.

Tharu women searching through aquatic vegetation for small fish.

A *cub of* Leopard 206.

They were twenty feet away, rolling, pouncing, dissolving into the grass, then reappearing. One of them left the others and crept, belly to the ground, to the water's edge to drink. While its tongue flicked the water, its eyes stared unblinkingly at my blind. I took a photograph and it stopped to glare at me; it already had the intent cat gaze that makes people nervous. There was barely enough light, so I moved the camera from the peephole and watched. Colors turned to gray and black, the other two cubs came to drink, and then a larger shape appeared—their mother.

The cubs bumped their heads against her chin and face, making small fluttering noises in their throats. She licked them roughly and carelessly, like a mother trying not to show too much affection to a teenager. I didn't notice her radio collar at first; the blue tape against the black radio collar was frayed and barely visible in the dusk, but she was 206, the Sauraha Leopard. We had captured her near the house after she had made several raids on our goat shed. She had obviously left her cubs for the day in this patch of grass near the river and they had remained there, still and silent, while the fishing women and I had talked and splashed only a few feet away.

This, it seems to me, is the essence of leopards, and maybe the reason they can survive in small, isolated pockets long after the other big cats are gone. Given half a chance, leopards are able to live next to villages, flocks, and fields. They can eat rabbits, barking deer, and village dogs, interspersed with goats and calves. They can lie up all day in the smallest, scrubbiest patch of cover while children herd goats and sheep all around them. They can switch from being active during the day to being completely nocturnal, and they can even mate and raise cubs in circumstances none of the other big cats would tolerate. However, their ability to live close to people has given rise to a false sense of security about the leopard's future.

Leopards have the widest geographical distribution of all the five species of big cats. They are found in a range of habitat types, from tropical forest to semiarid scrub, and are more tolerant of human activity than the tiger, lion, or jaguar. Although numerous reports and articles have been written on their habits and densities, there have been few studies of leopards in the wild and almost none that followed individually identifiable animals for any length of time.

Most of what is known of leopard reproduction comes from information collected in zoos. Even though the data may be influenced by captive conditions, it is illuminating and relevant to the leopard's survival in the wild. The most important point is that leopards seem to have fewer cubs per litter than the other big cats. Zoo data on more than two hundred litters shows an average litter size of two cubs for leopards compared with nearly three for tigers and three for lions. This might not seem like a big difference, but it adds up over the course of a female's reproductive lifetime.

Although only six leopards were radio collared during the eight-year tiger project in Chitwan, all of them were monitored until they died or disappeared. We found that leopards were much more difficult to catch than tigers; they were more wary and tended to sit tight rather than allow themselves to be driven in a particular direction. This meant we could not use the *bhit* cloth technique to catch them but had to lure them into traps baited with a live goat.

John Seidensticker and Kirti Tamang had captured the project's first leopard, known as 201, or the Patch One female. Her home range was completely inside the park and bordered the Rapti River. Two months after she was radio collared she gave birth to three cubs, and by monitoring the den site continuously John found that the female spent more than half her time away from her young. She would leave the cubs for as long as thirty-six hours, then return and spend a similar length of time with them. Before they were ten weeks old, one of the cubs disappeared, leaving two males who became 203 and 204 when Mel and Kirti radio collared them a year later.

In addition to the Patch One female, we had radio collars on two other leopards known as the Bodrani and Sauraha females. Both of their home ranges lay mostly outside the park boundaries and included agricultural land and scrub, interspersed with patches of short grassland used to graze village flocks. We had also noted the presence of a large, extremely wary male leopard who avoided our capture attempts, so we could not collect much information on his movements. However, judging by the frequency with which his tracks appeared at Sauraha, he roamed over a very large area. To our knowledge, his territory included the ranges of the two females living outside the park plus the Patch One female's range inside the park. His pugmarks were distinctive, almost the size of those of a small tigress, and on one occasion he killed a buffalo bait we had set out for a tiger on Itarni Island, something the female leopards never did.

Like a male tiger, the leopard made long, purposeful movements in a single night, never detouring from the path or stopping to rest. I followed his tracks one morning for three miles; he had walked along the north bank of the Rapti River, sometimes next to the water, sometimes along the narrow raised rim of the rice fields. His entire route edged cultivated land, and his tracks passed within a few yards of several houses and livestock pens. Two days later, he made the return trip by the same route.

The home range of the Patch One leopard overlapped extensively with the home range of the tigress we called Number One, but there were subtle differences in the way the two female cats used their areas. The tigress frequently used roads and trails, while the leopard rarely did so. There were also differences in the way the two cats used the grasslands after the annual burning. The leopard moved in almost immediately after the fires. She seemed to be hunting hog deer, which remained in the small patches of unburned grass. A few weeks after the fires, new grass shoots attracted large herds of chital and hog deer, but there was not enough stalking cover for the tigress, who continued to hunt in the forests. A month later the grass was three feet high, and the tigress shifted her movements into the grasslands while the leopard moved back into the forest.

Although a male leopard may occasionally take something bigger, most leopards' prey is in the fifty- to one hundred–pound range. Tigers' prey is larger, weighing one hundred to three hundred pounds, but Number One also killed sambar deer and some domestic stock weighing as much as nine hundred pounds. There was a small overlap in the diets of leopards and tigers, but in general they hunted different prey using slightly different stalk-and-ambush tactics.

Both cats are mainly nocturnal, but leopards seem to move less often and spend more time in each spot. Tigers also employed the move-and-stop hunting technique but never stayed as long as leopards in any one place. We spent many hours at night listening to the steady, motionless signal of a leopard, wondering what on earth it was doing. Leopards were so still during these periods of inactivity that they were almost certainly just sitting, watching, and listening. After an hour or so of waiting, they would move a short distance and wait again.

The two female leopards that lived outside the park preyed extensively on domestic stock. Three-quarters of their kills were cows, goats, sheep, or dogs, sometimes made during the day or late afternoon. At night we often sat by the fire listening to the radio signal from the Sauraha Leopard as she moved through the village in search of a meal. We could follow her progress not only by the radio signal but also by the barking and howling of village dogs.

The majority of leopards in Chitwan live on the edges of the park, either just inside or just outside the park boundary. Outside the park they survive where tigers cannot; within the park they manage to co-exist with the socially dominant tiger, mainly by avoiding hunting places and rest sites tigers prefer. To do this leopards need a supply of smaller prey and a vegetation type that enables them to avoid tigers. Sal forest covers more than three quarters of the interior of the park and fulfills neither of these requirements. It is open, sometimes parklike, and in it prey densities are low. So in Chitwan, at least, the leopards live on the edge, between people and tigers. Although they are more successful than tigers at surviving close to people, it may be that living with tigers is their best option.

The Bodrani Leopard was pregnant when we radio collared her. Later, while we tracked her, we saw her with a single small cub. She and the cub made their living in the hacked-over forest near the village of Bodrani, preying on sheep, goats, and chital deer. She never crossed the Rapti River into the Patch One leopard's territory but occasionally made excursions to Itarni Island near our house. One day her radio signal was different. It was strong, as if she was high in a tree, and coming from a place she had never been before, so Mel decided to investigate further.

That afternoon, he and two *shikaris* followed the signal through fields and around houses along the north bank of the Rapti River. As the houses got closer together, the signal became stronger and his entourage of curious onlookers grew. Mel says he felt a bit like the villain in a cowboy movie as he walked the main street of the village, pointing the antenna at houses while crowds of people followed at a discreet distance. At one point the signal faded, and he thought he had passed the leopard, but when he retreated a few paces the antenna pointed directly at a house. To be certain there was no mistake, Mel walked around the house and garden several times. Without a doubt, the leopard or its collar was inside. There was some agitated conversation among the crowd on the porch, a young man disappeared inside the house, and suddenly the radio signal changed: it was moving, slightly fainter. Mel walked around to the back to find that the signal was now coming from a haystack. Buried inside was the Bodrani Leopard's collar, intact. The collar could not have come off unless the leopard's head had come off too, so one of the *shikaris* asked what had happened to the animal. The houseowners said they had not killed the leopard but had found the collar close by. Close by were scrubby grazed forest, houses, and rice fields, so she had almost certainly been poisoned.

It is not difficult to poison a leopard or a tiger. When it kills one of your goats you pour insecticide or any other commonly available poison into the carcass, then wait for the animal to return to finish the kill. When the leopard returns to feed, it unknowingly eats the poison and dies, horribly, soon after.

That almost certainly had been the fate of the Bodrani female and later another uncollared female leopard who was actually heard dying near the Bhawanipur guardpost. The guards heard a commotion of thrashing and roaring that continued for over an hour, and when the noise finally stilled they went to investigate. A leopard lay dead in a patch of broken and shredded bushes. They brought her to our camp and we examined her body. She was a young animal in the prime of life. Her teeth were white and strong and she was pregnant, near term with three fetuses. Most disturbingly, her claws were bushed and ragged, unlike any we had seen in a captured leopard. In her final agony she must have raked the bushes and earth until her claws disintegrated.

It seems hard to place the subsistence farmer in the position of deciding how and when leopards should die, but throughout the leopard's world, farmers are the ones who make the final decision. Leopards do not have the power of lions or tigers to attract tourists, because by nature they are hard to see. They are lower on the list of exciting animals to photograph. Rumor has it that they are in no danger compared with tigers, but they are not doing as well as many people think.

Certainly in Chitwan, one of the premier national parks of Asia, they are not doing as well as one would suppose. Five of the seven leopards we observed or radio collared died of poisoning or unknown causes before they reached old age. Other leopards did not fill the gaps these dead leopards left for long periods of time, suggesting that there were few other leopards out there looking for a place to live.

Leopards can coexist with lions or tigers, and they can survive in seriously disturbed areas that would not support a tiger, but because they adapt readily to feeding on livestock they are very susceptible to poisoning. To that, they can never adapt.

8   Tiger Moon

*T*HE TIGERS IN CHITWAN were active during the hours of darkness and well into the morning. Most of them rested between eleven in the morning and midafternoon, although after an unsuccessful night's hunting they were sometimes active for most of the day. During the hot season they often spent the midday hours resting in water along shallow streams or at the edge of a *tal*. An hour before sunset they were on the move again, and their activity patterns reflected those of the deer they hunted.

A *tiger cooling itself at midday.*

To find out just what tigers were doing at night, we had to be out there with them. At the other end of the park, Chuck McDougal managed to follow nightly movements by backtracking pugmarks, and we used the same technique whenever we could. However, many of our study animals ranged over areas lacking the sandy trails or riverbeds that would show pugmarks, so radio tracking was the only way we could monitor many of the tigers. We either drove up and down the road taking compass bearings every half hour on two or more neighboring tigers, or Mel sat up in a tall tree all night and monitored a single animal. The tall-tree technique was dangerous in thunderstorms and did not provide nearly as much information, so most of the data we collected at night were taken from the relative safety of a vehicle. But we could not time our night samples randomly, as science dictates; rather, we were dependent upon whether the Green Latrine was starting and running well. During the day there were always plenty of people around to help push-start the vehicle, but at night, with only the two of us, starting it was a different matter. Our major worry was that some night the Green Latrine would quit, leaving us stranded miles from anywhere.

We began our preparations for these nightly expeditions by three-thirty each afternoon, making sandwiches and flasks of coffee. The Green Latrine sulked if asked to ford the river too often, so we usually left it inside the park at the edge of the river and took a boat to wherever it was parked. Kancha Lama helped us carry the baggage down to the river and load it into the dugout canoe. Even though he wasn't driving, Kancha Lama usually accompanied us at the outset of these nocturnal expeditions. He had a special rapport with the vehicle that bordered on the metaphysical, a rapport expressed through bouquets of sharp-smelling marigolds and much tightening of nuts and bolts. I don't think Kancha Lama was ever completely convinced of our ability to survive a drive through the park without him, and he always parted with the vehicle reluctantly, like an anxious father lending his car on a Saturday night.

As we set out, the grasslands were glistening gold, the evening light exaggerating their beauty to an intensity that was almost a physical sensation. Peacocks' cries floated back and forth across the landscape as they settled their exorbitant plumage into the trees, and flocks of ibis flew through the bright sky toward their roosts. The almost-full moon was high in the sky as the sun set and the light silvered, moving day into night without its ever really getting dark. There was not likely to be any traffic, so we coasted to a stop in the middle of the road and sat on the roof without speaking, listening to the zoom and buzz of the night sounds.

Mel checked the radio frequencies of tigers in the vicinity, and we waited. Plump bats flickered above us, snapping at insects, and the moon cast a neon light on the silver-black landscape. It was light enough to see, but brown moving against green became black on black; we were robbed of our daytime advantage. Sounds compensated for the lack of color. We were intensely aware of the small noises in the grass, a mouse, a cricket, our own breathing. Sound became the primary sense, alerting us to movement.

A distant smashing noise came closer; something heavy was moving through the vegetation toward us. I wondered if perhaps we'd be better off inside the Jeep as a large black shape emerged onto the road ahead. It was a sloth bear, going about its nightly business of finding food. We watched quietly from the roof as it sniffed the front tire like a dog, then wandered round us and continued down the road. We could hear its snuffling breaths fifty yards away.

The radio signals from Tigress Number One and the Roaring Tigress were coming in loud and clear, but no one else was close enough to be heard. The Roaring Tigress was still sexually immature and sharing her mother's range, but the two were hunting in different areas about a mile apart. Judging from their intermittent radio signals, both tigresses were active but not moving far in terms of distance; they seemed to be intensively hunting small patches of forest, and their bouts of activity were interspersed with long periods when we could detect no movement at all. It was as if they had chosen a likely ambush spot and settled down to wait.

The night chilled, and we began to feel cold and drowsy. Every half hour Mel and I took turns unraveling ourselves from our respective blankets, climbed out of the vehicle, and carried the antenna and receiver a few yards down the road to listen for signals and take compass bearings. Then in a flurry of activity we would start the Jeep, drive a measured distance down the road, and take another set of bearings. After plotting the positions of the two tigresses on an aerial photograph, we waited another half hour and repeated the process. It was monotonous work, punctuated only by cups of coffee, gluey peanut butter sandwiches, and conversation.

After the eleven-thirty compass bearings, Mel returned to the Jeep slightly more animated than usual. "Get ready to move," he said, "I think Number One's decided to call it a night for that area. She's moving out fast." Half an hour later, Number One had traveled almost two miles, and we guessed she was walking along a well-used trail that ran between the forest and a grassy area known as Simul Gol. "Must remember to check the trail for tracks before we go back to camp in the morning," Mel said, more enthusiastic now that something was happening. Every piece of information we gathered on the tigers' nightly movements was valuable, but sitting for twelve hours listening to a stationary signal as a tiger fed on a kill and rested afterward was unbelievably soporific. It was always a relief to be kept busy during a night sample and much easier to stay awake if something was happening.

Number One moved toward Simul Gol at a fairly rapid pace. She was walking toward the main park road and our vehicle, so her signal grew louder and louder. I wondered if she would turn and come right past us, but Mel thought she was just moving between hunting areas. Through following the tigers at night we had learned that females in particular hunted an area for several hours, then moved to another area some distance away. Sometimes a tigress moved soon after we had heard deer alarm calls from her vicinity, while at other times the tigress seemed to just give up and decide another hunting ground might be more profitable. Either explanation seemed plausible in this case, as we had been too far away to hear if the deer had been spooked. Whatever the reasons for their moves, hunting tigresses seemed to choose a destination before they moved, for they rarely wandered around in circles when moving from one hunting area to the next. Instead, they walked quite rapidly along a road or trail, as if they had a mental map of all the good hunting areas within their range and the most direct routes to them.

Simul Gol was obviously the place Number One had decided upon for her next hunting spot, for she stopped on the edge of the trees and settled in to wait. It was a favorite hunting area, and we had previously found several of her chital and sambar kills there. A narrow swath of tall, swampy grasses bordered by higher, drier ground cut between two patches of forest. The boundary between forest and grass was abrupt, marked by six-foot banks in many places, and the area looked as if it had once been an oxbow lake or *tal*. Several major trails meandered through the thick grasses, and it was probably a good place to wait for deer and pigs crossing between the two patches of forest.

Shortly after Number One arrived at Simul Gol, the Roaring Tigress began to move too. She crossed a small stream and walked away from us toward the main Rapti River, keeping to the edge of the forest. Then, to our surprise, she turned and seemed to be walking straight down the park road toward us, making a half circle from where she had started.

By two in the morning, both tigresses were in Simul Gol, within a few hundred yards of each other. We parked on the main road a short distance away while Mel sat quietly on the roof of the Jeep, listening to their signals. It looked like a chance mother-daughter encounter, but what would they do? Nothing? Pass each other with a greeting? Fight? It would be difficult to tell from the radio signals alone. Once again we cursed the darkness and thick vegetation, wishing we had a magic way of "seeing" through them.

We were close enough to hear grass rustle when the tigresses moved, and for a few seconds there was commotion—a rush, struggling, then a tremendous woofing roar, deafeningly close. Instantly Mel was off the roof and beside the Jeep, the half-open door between him and the noise. I was frozen by the unexpectedness of the enormous sound. The sporadic, thrashing noise of a struggle began again, accompanied by a series of shattering roars. Both tigresses were roaring now, angry, thunderous blasts of sound that resonated through our bodies. It was overwhelming, like sitting in front of a loudspeaker or being physically shaken by a strong wind. Between the bouts of roaring came a softer but somehow even more frightening sound, the deep, stentorian breathing of two winded tigresses.

"Are they fighting?" I managed to whisper to Mel, who by now was sitting inside the Jeep, holding the antenna rather unnecessarily out of the window. The earphones were hanging loosely around his neck, and I could hear the loud, splatting noise of a strong radio signal. "I don't know," he replied, "but it sounds like a hell of a struggle." The confusion of roars and crashing noises continued for what seemed like hours but by real time was only twenty minutes. When I finally relaxed, my ears were ringing and I was exhausted, euphoric, as if I'd survived a cyclone. Mel was the first to recover. He stepped out of the vehicle to listen to the radio signals. The tigers were only fifty yards from the road, and so close to each other that he couldn't distinguish between the two signals. We waited immobile and silent for an hour or more, checking the receiver at ten-minute intervals. The intermittent signals indicated that the tigresses were active, but they were not moving.

A well-tutored ear can distinguish movement from a seemingly stationary radio signal because a small head movement by a collared animal changes the orientation of the collar. This causes the signal to alter slightly in strength and interval, in the same way that a signal changes when an animal is walking past trees and other obstacles. When a signal alters like this, and the animal's position does not change, it generally indicates grooming or feeding. By three-thirty in the morning neither of the tigresses had moved much, but we continued to get the same mysterious activity signals from their radio collars. As things had become comparatively quiet at Simul Gol, we decided to move on and try to locate some of the other tigers.

Trees closed around us in the lurching headlights, and a sambar leaped across the road, leaving puffs of dust hanging in the air where its hooves hit the ground. Relying on their camouflage, nightjars waited until the last possible second before flying out from under the wheels of the Jeep. All around us the leaves were decorated with millions of tiny lights that sparkled like minute jewels; when we stopped to look more closely with a flashlight, they turned out to be the reflections of a multitude of spider eyes.

Further on, near the Dumaria guardpost, we paused to listen for other tigers. From the south, toward the Siwalik Hills, we heard a faint, distant signal from the Sauraha male, while from the west in the direction we were driving, came the somewhat stronger signal of the Jarneli Tigress. Mel sat on the roof and searched for radio signals as I drove slowly down the narrow track with only the sidelights on. A herd of chital standing in chest-deep grass turned their soft faces toward us. They looked different at night, like dappled, imaginary creatures, curious but not alarmed by the mechanical intruder. A doe raised her muzzle and alarm whooped tentatively, almost testing, to see what the rest of the herd thought. Others called in return, and the group bounded off in slow motion, leaping dreamily through the silver grass.

The patchy forest opened out into a large circular area of short grass that was a favorite afternoon feeding place of gaur and chital. Now only an owl silently quartered the empty field. The landscape was a gleaming monochrome engraving, dark hills framed the dew-spangled meadow, and trees clustered like groups of people knee-deep in mist. The owl swung away abruptly as a shape stirred on the edge of the forest. The shape moved deliberately, not with the jerky, stop-start motion of a deer, and although I couldn't see it clearly I knew it had to be a cat.

It was the Jarneli Tigress. Trailed by a long moonshadow, she strolled across the grass, then paused, lowered her head, and roared twice, "Arr-angh, arr-angh," a hollow, melancholy sound. She walked on, not stopping to listen for an answer, just calling mournfully into the night. The outline of her body flickered and disappeared as she brushed through wisps of fog, but we could hear her echoing calls long after she was gone. Although I should have been excited by the unexpected pleasure of seeing this glorious creature, I was left with an inexplicable sense of sadness and loss, almost as if I had just seen the last tigress on earth. We sat there for a long time listening to her signal, then started back toward camp.

At dawn the wailing howls of jackals rose and fell around us, sobbing like mourners at a grave. The moon had set, and the earlier shades of gray and silver were gone, leaving a thick, fog-saturated darkness impervious to headlights. It was as if the moon and mist had conspired to make us suddenly blind. We decided to call it a night and drove slowly along the road, more to avoid bumping into rhinos than to avoid taking a wrong turn. Ahead, the plodding outline of an elephant appeared with a small, blanket-shrouded figure perched on its neck. Day had begun, and one of the government elephants was setting out to collect fodder. The elephant moved to the side of the road as we passed and reached out its trunk toward the Jeep, feeling the air for scent.

Back at Simul Gol, we listened for the Roaring Tigress and her mother. They were some distance away from the site of the earlier struggle and about four hundred yards apart. We debated whether to go in and look at the area. Mel was all in favor of a quick examination of the site, but I thought it might be dangerous and suggested we go back to camp and return on an elephant. The argument was just becoming heated when the solution to our problem, two more government elephants, came walking down the road.

From elephant back the site of the struggle stood out like a helicopter landing pad: large area of flattened grass, tufts of hair, spots of blood, then off to one side the carcass of a young male sambar. Although the mess made it difficult to decipher the course of events, the deer's deep footprints and scattered hair led us to believe that the two tigresses had had a hard time killing this particular sambar. We had assumed we'd heard a fight between the two tigresses, but now it seemed as if the commotion had been the two cats trying to kill the sambar. Judging from the tracks at the carcass, both tigresses had fed and left, maybe because they were disturbed by the elephants going by on the road a few feet away. The tigresses must have been feeding while we listened to their stationary but active radio signals. It did not seem as if they had set out to cooperate in making the kill, but chance had put them both in the same place at the same time. It was an unusual situation, but it did demonstrate that even older, experienced hunters like Number One do not always find it easy to kill a large animal like a sambar.

In our eagerness to find out what had transpired between the tigresses in the dark, we had made a mistake. Asking a government elephant driver to help search for a tiger kill was like sending out invitations to a feast. Once the drivers knew where the sambar carcass was, there was nothing we could do except collect the lower jaw. The tigresses lost their hard-won meal to the government elephant camp and would have to kill again soon. Forty or more people would dine on sambar meat tonight, and we would hear the sounds of singing and dancing well into the evening as the elephant drivers celebrated their lucky find.

For some tigresses, losing kills to meat-starved people was a serious problem. Most of the poaching was done by the elephant drivers while they were out cutting fodder for their elephants. Usually they stumbled upon the kills accidentally but sometimes, if a particularly noisy kill occurred within earshot of their camp, the *hatizar* or government elephant camp would gather up several of the old tiger-hunting elephants and set out to drive the tiger off its meal before it had had a chance to eat too much. This practice certainly meant that tigers had to kill more often and probably made a great deal of difference to females trying to feed large hungry cubs.

Every tiger kill we found provided a wealth of useful information: weight, sex, age, and species, as well as where it was killed, and how. We discovered that tigers use two major methods of killing prey. Smaller animals are killed with a bite to the nape of the neck; the cervical vertebrae are often crushed or damaged, and death probably results from damage to the central nervous system. Large prey are killed with a throat bite, and the tiger maintains its hold for several minutes, essentially suffocating the animal. There was an interesting relationship between the weight of the tiger, the size of the prey, and the method the tiger used to make the kill. When the prey was less than half the weight of the tiger, the tiger used a nape bite to kill. Animals more than half the weight of the tiger were killed with a throat bite. Young, inexperienced tigers used a throat bite more often, regardless of the size of the prey. It may be that the throat bite is less dangerous for the tiger or requires less precise orientation of the canines, because Chuck McDougal found that as young tigers gained experience at killing, they tended to use the nape-bite technique more often.

Like all cats, a hunting tiger relies upon surprise. Our night tracking data showed that tigers often hunt while moving slowly along roads and trails. These natural travel routes allow them to move quietly, without pushing through heavy brush and grasses. The trails are often used by deer and pigs as well, so the chances of encountering prey are high. At other times tigers seem to choose a likely spot and wait, perhaps for a herd of grazing deer to move closer. The tigers we followed definitely had favorite hunting areas that they visited regularly. However, once a tiger had made an unsuccessful attempt at a kill it usually gave up and moved to a different hunting area; all the deer in Chitwan have loud,

The tiger is a formidable predator.

penetrating alarm calls that almost certainly alert potential prey in the vicinity.

Stalking tigers make full use of every tiny piece of cover. They crouch behind small bushes, rocks, and trees, or hug the edge of a riverbank. Only when you watch a tiger stalk or move slowly through the grass can you fully appreciate the effectiveness of its striped coat. Patterns of gold and black break up its body outline, and in moonlight or even midday a tiger merges with the background so completely that you can stare at it for minutes without really seeing the whole animal. A hunting tiger has infinite patience. It will wait an hour for a deer to come close enough, or spend fifteen mintues stalking twenty yards. The final rush is an explosion of power; once a tiger is committed, there is only speed and concentration.

The first strike is usually on the prey's hindquarters or body, and the main effort is to bring the prey down or into a position where the killing bite can be delivered. It is a dangerous moment. Deer have slashing hooves and antlers, while pigs have thick, muscular bodies and sharp tusks. Even with the advantage of surprise, the tiger risks a disabling injury. Speed, experience, concentration, and judgment are at a premium. Everything must mesh for the tiger to be successful; only an estimated one hunt in twenty results in a kill.

If the kill is made in an open area, the tiger usually drags the carcass into nearby cover before it starts to feed. The distance varies from a few feet to several miles, depending on the place, the tiger's mood, or any number of unidentified reasons. We once followed the tracks of the Sauraha Tiger after he had dragged and carried a dead buffalo for six hundred yards before he found a satisfactory dining place. There are some impressive records of tigers carrying their prey over long distances; Jim Corbett once saw a tiger carry a full-grown cow for more than four miles.

A tiger almost invariably begins feeding on the rump of a carcass, eating its way toward the abdomen and forequarters. A feeding tiger can consume prodigious quantities of meat. Number One once ate nearly seventy pounds, or about a fifth of her body weight, in less than twenty-four hours. However, the average amount tigers eat per day at a

A tigress stalking through tall grass shows how effective her striped coat is as camouflage; the white spots on the backs of her ears may serve as signals to her cubs.

kill is about thirty-three pounds; their general daily average is about ten to twelve pounds. Larger animals like sambar and buffalo provide food for several days, and tigers usually remain near their kills, alternately feeding and resting until the carcass is reduced to bones and skin. In a rather extravagant killing spree, the Sauraha Tiger once dispatched a cow and a buffalo that had wandered into the park. The carcasses lay close together, a few feet from the main park road. The Sauraha Tiger fed on them for four days; then, after he left, the Jarneli Tigress and her two large cubs came and ate. In all, the four tigers ate nearly four hundred and forty pounds of meat in seven days.

Presumably, tigers remain near their kills to protect them from scavengers. Wild pigs, vultures, jackals, jungle cats, and even crocodiles have been seen scavenging at tiger kills; but competition from scavengers does not seem to be so intense for tigers as it is for lions, which live in more open habitats where kills are easily found by vultures, hyenas, and other lions.

We used a combination of two different methods to find out exactly what prey species the tigers were feeding on. Whenever we found kills that were fresh, we checked the physical condition of the animal, weighed it, and collected the lower jaw so it could be aged later by tooth sectioning. Kills that were several days old did not provide as much information, but we still identified the species and collected the lower jaw. This method overestimated the number of larger animals in the tigers' diets, because we were more likely to find those kills at which tigers spent more time.

To compensate, we also collected scats, or feces, as a convenient but slightly smelly way of studying a tiger's diet. Once we dried and washed scats, we could separate out the hair, bones, teeth, and claws of whatever the tiger had last eaten. Remains of a variety of smaller animals showed up in the fecal samples, including hares, langur monkeys, civets, and porcupines. Although they prefer larger prey, tigers will take whatever they can kill, and some of the more outlandish reports from the old hunting literature include tigers feeding on frogs, locusts, crabs, and crocodiles.

In general, the tiger's diet consisted mainly of deer; of the four deer species in Chitwan, tigers seemed to prefer sambar, killing them out of proportion to their abundance. When we analyzed the teeth in the deer jaws, we found that tigers were not killing just old, very young, or sick prey; they took a broad spectrum of animals, including prime, healthy adults. This random selection reflects the tiger's hunting style. Predators like wolves and wild dogs, which chase their prey, might be expected to single out less fit animals that cannot stay the course during a long chase, but stalk-and-ambush hunters such as tigers take whatever happens to be accessible and vulnerable at the moment.

Early in the study we realized that the Chitwan tigers rarely spent more than a single day at a rest site before moving on to another portion of their range. When they remained in the same place for more than a day, we assumed they had made a kill, noted their position, and searched the area after they had left. Almost always we found the remains of something they had been feeding on, so we had a fairly accurate measure of how often tigers made a large kill. We had no way of telling how often they killed smaller animals like monkeys or peafowl because these would be a quick snack, consumed in minutes rather than hours.

Tigress Number One made a large kill once very eight days when she had only herself to feed, but her rate rose to one kill every five or six days when she had two six-month-old cubs to provide for. Other tigresses followed the same pattern. During a year, a single tiger would need to make forty to fifty large kills, and a tigress with young would need sixty to seventy-five. It is difficult to assess what effect this level of predation is having on prey species in Chitwan, but we know that over a six-year period chital numbers have increased markedly, while populations of sambar, hog deer, and barking deer have remained about the same. During this same period, tiger numbers have remained fairly constant, suggesting that predation by tigers has not limited prey populations in the long term.

Our night tracking sessions made it obvious that tigers spent most of their time hunting in riverine forest and grassland habitats, not surprising given that there were four times as many deer in these areas as in sal forest. The high density of deer in these habitats translates into high tiger density, and the flood plain grasslands and riverine forests of Chitwan support one adult tiger per eight square miles, the highest tiger densities ever recorded. Clearly preservation of these habitats is the key to the tiger's long-term survival in Nepal.

9   The Roaring Tigress

I WOKE WITH A START and lay under the mosquito net, wondering what had roused me from sleep. All I could hear were the usual sounds—frogs calling, the Scops owl above our house, and Mel's breathing beside me. We had gone to bed at the usual time the night before, and nothing had seemed different.

Then I heard it again, the ghostly alarm calls of chital deer. Again and again the calls sounded, each closer and more urgent. I woke Mel, and we lay listening. The deer were obviously reacting to a predator, so we took radio-tracking gear and ran through the frequencies of all the radio-collared tigers and leopards to see if any animal we knew was causing the panic. After a few moments, one signal came through so loud and clear that I could hear it without headphones. It was the Roaring Tigress, a few hundred yards away at most, and as I peered into the blackness I half expected to see her. I wondered what she was doing so close to the houses.

At that moment all hell broke loose among the elephants. They swung their chains, screaming shrill, frantic blasts of fright and warning into the dark. The elephant men scrambled from their beds, shouting commands to the trembling beasts, trying to soothe them with familiar orders. Mel disappeared down the steps into the night, carrying the radio-tracking gear. "She's still right there behind the elephants," he said as he went over to tell the *shikaris* and elephant men the reason for the disturbance. Gradually, the elephant noises diminished to a low grumble, and I went back to bed while Mel sat on the porch following the tigress by the sound of her radio signal.

An hour later he woke me. "She's at it again. Come and listen to this," he said excitedly, but outside there were only the normal night sounds. If anything, it seemed quieter than usual. Then "Ahhaa-oon, ahhaa-oon, ahhaa-oon"—a deep, hollow resonant call spread and echoed across the miles of dark forest, impossibly, unnaturally loud.

123

The hairs on the backs of our necks stood up, and the jittery peacocks miaowed nervously back and forth to one another from their roosts. This was the sixth night in a row that the tigress had roared like this. Although her identification number was 103, we had named her the Roaring Tigress about three months earlier when she had first begun calling. At that time she was two-and-a-half years old and coming into heat for the first time.

The Roaring Tigress and her brother, Tiger 104, were offspring of the large tigress we called Number One, who lived just across the river from our camp. The two cubs had been born in an area of dense, tall grass near a small stream. They weighed only two or three pounds when they were born after the short, fifteen-week gestation period, but they put on weight rapidly in their first month. They first opened their eyes when they were two weeks old but continued to feed solely on their mother's milk for several more weeks. During the first few weeks of the cubs' lives, Number One spent most of her time at the den with them, leaving only for short periods to drink or hunt. While her cubs were restricted to the den site, her home range was dramatically reduced to less than a quarter of its former size, a pattern shown by all tigresses in the first few months after the birth of their cubs.

Although tiger cubs have a full set of milk teeth when they are a month old, they do not begin to eat solid food until they are six to eight weeks old. At that point their mother starts to lead them to kills she makes near the den.

Male cubs seem to grow faster and learn to kill on their own more quickly than females. When the Roaring Tigress and Tiger 104 were both eighteen months of age, she weighed two hundred and fifty pounds and her brother was a hundred pounds heavier. At that point both cubs were still using their mother's home range but spending long periods of time away from her. They shared several kills and spent more time with each other than they did with their mother. A month later, Tiger 104 started exploring. While the Roaring Tigress continued to use only her mother's eight-square-mile range, within a few months Tiger 104 had expanded his horizons and was covering eighteen square miles, ranging over almost exactly the same area as his father. Father and son shared the same piece of ground quite amicably, and in the hot season we often found them resting within a few hundred yards of each other in the thick, cool grass around the oxbow lake known as Majur Tal.

The age at which young tigers disperse from their natal or birth areas seems to vary from between eighteen months to two and a half years, depending largely on when their mother gives birth to a new litter. In his study of tiger dispersal, Dave Smith found that young tigers disperse two to three months after a new litter is born, timing that coincides almost exactly with when the new cubs will leave the den site and begin to follow their mother around.

When the Roaring Tigress and her brother were eighteen months old, their mother mated again with their father, the Sauraha Tiger. The cubs were born three and a half months later; strangely, the Roaring Tigress was with her mother or very close by when she gave birth. When she was two years old, the Roaring Tigress moved out of her mother's range, but she did not go far. She set up residence on the small island of Itarni, on the edge of her mother's range and a few hundred yards from our camp. Although the island measured only about one square mile, it was covered by dense, impenetrable riverine forest surrounded by short grasses. Full of sambar, chital, and wild boar, it was unoccupied by other tigers and rarely disturbed by people, despite the fact that it lay so close to the edge of the park. The Roaring Tigress confined herself to this small area, occasionally crossing the Rapti River to visit the boundaries of her mother's range. Six months after she had moved out of her mother's home range, the Roaring Tigress began calling and earned her name.

We dressed hurriedly against the cold, foggy night and headed for the main bullock-cart ford, where Mel thought we'd have the best chance of hearing the Sauraha Tiger's radio signal if he chose this night to respond to the calls of the Roaring Tigress. The walk to the river crossing was an easy stroll in the middle of the afternoon, but at night it was another world. Moonlight spun the fog into pale, drifting shapes, and every sound was startlingly loud. A rhino cow and calf stared dreamily at us, then continued their loud munching. We climbed the steps of the old, deserted guardpost near the crossing and settled down to wait.

For an hour and a half, nothing happened. Then the chital announced the tigress's presence, filling the air suddenly with their high, flutey alarm calls and sounds of panicked running feet. Their panic was contagious; I felt as if I should be escaping with them in this dark world of mist, where sounds were the only clue to what was going on. The tigress's radio signal indicated that she was on the same side of the river as we were; we had walked right past her. The signal grew stronger and stronger as the tigress walked along the riverbank toward us. Then, a faint splashing noise. I nudged Mel, who with the headphones on was deaf to all but the radio signal. The tigress was crossing the Dhungri River toward the park; then the earth-shattering roars began again.

The noise was so loud that the air trembled. Her long, drawn-out, moaning calls resounded across the flood plain again and again, twenty or thirty times. Then, suddenly, we heard a distant answering roar, faint by comparison but very clear. Mel tuned in the Sauraha Tiger's frequency. His signal was coming from inside the park, and judging from its strength he was at least a mile away. Over the next half hour his radio signal got stronger and his answering roars grew louder, until the Sauraha Tiger stood on the other side of the Rapti River. The Roaring Tigress and Sauraha Tiger called back and forth to one another in a powerful, thundering duet. He swam across the river to meet her and followed her onto the island.

Early the next morning we backtracked the events of the previous night, following the pugmarks of the Roaring Tigress. She had come along the riverbank and crossed the narrow Dhungri River to the western point of Itarni Island, where she had stood to roar her summons into the night. The broad pugmarks of the Sauraha Tiger had come straight down the park road, and after emerging from the river, they had joined hers as the tigers crossed the broad sandy floodplain of the island. In places the tigers had walked side by side forty or fifty yards apart, and at other times he obviously had followed her closely. They spent two days together, then he left but returned three weeks later and again two weeks after that. Each time his visit lasted only two days.

When the Roaring Tigress finally became sexually mature, she clarified several aspects of tiger behavior for us. She had moved out of her mother's range several months prior to her first heat period, into an area that was not included in the Sauraha Tiger's home range. In fact, there did not seem to be a resident male who regularly visited the island. We were certain it was her roaring that had attracted the Sauraha Tiger's attention, for we had never found him there prior to her bouts of calling. Once he found her, he incorporated the island into his home range and began to visit her regularly.

Despite the fact that the Sauraha Tiger began to include her in his regular rounds, the Roaring Tigress did not conceive until nine months after her first heat period. This finding supports some of the evidence from zoos, which suggests that when a male and female meet there may be a period of familiarization before successful matings can take place. Like most members of the cat family, tigers show a great deal of ritualized threat behavior before and after mating. Zoo studies and the few rare glimpses of wild tigers consorting have shown that courtship is a noisy and dangerous activity, involving a lot of advance and retreat on the part of both participants.

In the wild, resident male tigers may meet and perhaps share an occasional kill with tigresses who live within their home ranges. They get to know one another and may even become quite friendly. However, this acquaintance probably develops over a long period of time and depends on the temperaments of the individuals involved.

Before the Roaring Tigress reached sexual maturity, we had never found her with the Sauraha Tiger. We could not be certain she was avoiding him, but ninety percent of the time they were over a mile apart whenever we located them. As soon as she came into heat, things changed, and we began to find them either together or within a few hundred yards of each other every time she showed signs of being in heat. The process of familiarization had begun.

The cubs born to Number One just before the Roaring Tigress moved out did not survive long. After they were born, Mel spent much of his time sitting in a tree a few hundred yards from the den. With the aid of the radio-tracking gear, he monitored how much time Number One spent with her new cubs, and she was there almost continuously, night and day, with only an occasional short hunting trip away from them.

One afternoon when the cubs were two weeks old and Number One was off on one of her short forays, Mel heard voices. A short time later he saw smoke and heard the crackling roar of a grass fire. Some villagers had illegally set fire to the area, and the wind was moving flames and smoke toward the den. If Number One had been there she might have had time to move the cubs, but she was off hunting, too far away to sense the threat. Heedless of the danger and scientific rules about not interfering in the lives of wild animals, Mel rushed in through the smoke. He knew only roughly where the den was, and it took him twenty minutes of mad searching to find it. There were three cubs, eyes not yet open, untouched by the flames but already dead, suffocated by the smoke. Cursing the arsonists that set the fire Mel wrapped their sturdy little bodies in his shirt and brought them back to camp.

Sadly, we weighed and measured them. They were all males, well fed and fat as butter. "What a waste," Mel murmured, his voice tight with anger, as he set off toward the guardpost to report the deaths. Of course the villagers who had set the fire were never found; it would have been an almost impossible task.

Seventeen days later Number One came into heat again. That night, tracks showed that the Sauraha Tiger had followed her for nearly a mile down the main park road, and they spent the following day together. Although she came into heat several times, Number One did not become pregnant again until four months after her litter had perished in the fire. She gave birth in mid-December, in the exact same place where she had borne the previous ill-fated litter. For a month all went well. However, with the onset of the grass-cutting season in January, thousands of villagers poured into the park. Despite our warnings that there was a tigress with cubs in the area, they continued to harvest grass near the den site. Impatient with their intrusions, Tigress Number One charged and threatened the villagers. Four times in as many days she rushed from the den, roaring and growling, but the grass cutters always returned. Finally she grew tired of the disturbance and moved the young to a distant corner of her range, well away from the noise of people.

It must have taken her all night to move the cubs the two miles to her new den site; the cubs were only a month old and certainly could not have walked that far by themselves. For the next month she stayed close to them, hunting nearby and confining her activities to a small area around the den site. She was absorbed in tending her young while her older daughter, the Roaring Tigress, continued to call for a mate.

It was such a gradual process that we hardly noticed what was happening. Night after night we plotted the Roaring Tigress' radio locations, looking for patterns or some unusual move. We were engrossed in the increasingly regular visits the Sauraha Tiger made to her at Itarni Island. Unlike studies in which you can watch an animal all day, ours was a guessing game of anticipation. What might the Roaring Tigress do next? Where should we concentrate our efforts so as not to miss a crucial piece of information? One night as we sat in the office, looking at range maps and aerial photographs by the glare of the hissing kerosene lantern, we suddenly recognized a change in her movements. During the past week the Roaring Tigress had spent more time in Number One's range than she had in the previous three months. We searched for a pattern in the daily locations, and it emerged, blindingly obvious. While Number One was confined to a small area with her young cubs, her daughter, the Roaring Tigress, was in the process of appropriating her mother's home range.

During the next two months the Roaring Tigress moved further and further into her mother's range, and by March she was spending all her time there. She no longer used Itarni Island but hunted and rested in the area where she had been born. Number One meantime made a few short forays back into the area that used to be her range, but it was too late. By March all her movements were confined to the periphery of her old range, and she had obviously lost her cubs, for we found her consorting with the Sauraha Tiger again. Clearly, her daughter had taken over.

During March, April, and May, Tigress Number One wandered back and forth along the boundaries of her old range. In May she made a few probes into the Jarneli Tigress' range to the west. Number One and the Jarneli Tigress had been neighbors for at least two years, but neither of them had ever trespassed on the other's territory before. While Number One was in the Jarneli Tigress' range, she killed a buffalo bait, and we darted her to change her collar. Her teeth and coat looked great, and she was in fine physical condition. We wondered what she would do next.

Meanwhile her daughter, the Roaring Tigress, had settled in. She took over her mother's range down to almost the exact same boundaries, mated successfully with the Sauraha Tiger, and in October bore her first cubs in the same thicket near the Tractor Bridge where her mother had previously given birth to at least two litters. Later, Dave Smith found that Tigress Number One had established a new home range in the sal forest adjoining her daughter's southern boundary. Number One successfully raised another litter and lived in her new range for three years, until she was poisoned by villagers.

We followed the progression of the range takeover with intense interest, monitoring both Number One and the Roaring Tigress closely. Apart from giving us a fascinating glimpse of how ranges change hands, the event raised some intriguing theoretical questions concerning home-range inheritance. Was this just a serendipitous occurrence or something that happened frequently between mothers and daughters? Did Number One move to accommodate her daughter, or did the Roaring Tigress appropriate the area?

Daughters in most mammal species tend to remain in their natal or birth areas. Some of the clearest results have come from Lynn Rogers' decade-long study of black bears in Minnesota. He found that one-and-a-half- to two-year-old independent bears restricted their activities to a small part of their mother's home range, while she used a different portion. After their second winter, most of the young males left, while the daughters expanded their activities within what had once been their mother's home range. It seemed that black bear mothers simply avoided using the sections of their home ranges that were occupied by their daughters and essentially "gave" them portions of their home ranges. All the social interactions that

Rogers witnessed were amicable, and because daughters were considerably smaller than their mothers, it seemed not to be a matter of daughters forcing mothers out.

Was this happening with tigers? Once we recognized what was going on between the two tigresses, we concentrated most of our efforts on their day-to-day movements. Although the range shift was a gradual process, at no time did it seem as if Number One had simply abandoned her range and donated it to her daughter. Rather, it was as if the Roaring Tigress had taken advantage of her mother's confinement with the new litter of cubs to claim ownership of the area.

In tiger terms, the exclusive rights to an area seem to belong to the individual who manages to get around and renew scent marks regularly. Because she moved her litter to a remote corner of her range and was confined to a small area around the den site while the cubs were very young, Number One was unable to get to all the borders to scent mark. Constantly probing these borders, the Roaring Tigress began to discover that "occupied" signs were fading and gradually moved further and further in. She was already familiar with the area, having grown up there. Why Number One finally relinquished the furthest portion of her range remains a mystery, but this event coincided with the loss of her cubs, and she subsequently began to wander.

Later, after our study had ended, Dave Smith and Chuck McDougal found this scenario repeated among other tigresses in other parts of the park. Another daughter completely took over her mother's range, and four other tigresses from different litters managed to squeeze in next to their mother. H. R. Panwar also observed similar events among tigresses in Kanha National Park in India.

If most tigresses settle next to their mothers, then it is almost as if they illustrate an early stage of lion society. Lions are the only cats that form permanent social groups, and a lioness and her grown daughters are the stable core of a pride. All the females in a pride are closely related. Mothers, daughters, sisters, and aunts usually stay in the pride where they were born, while young males leave when they become sexually mature. It seems a short step in evolutionary terms from mother and daughter living in adjoining or overlapping ranges to the beginnings of a pride composed of closely related females.

Until recently, the most usual explanation for the lions' uncatlike social behavior has been drawn from their unique habit of cooperative hunting. Biologists had speculated that because a pride of lions is able to bring down larger game or work together to ambush game in a fairly open environment, lions find it to their advantage to live in groups. However, Craig Packer, who with Anne Pusey has made extensive studies of lions in the Serengeti, has recently reanalyzed twenty years of lion data and come up with a new interpretation. He has found that lions living in large prides actually have a lower level of food intake than lions living in smaller prides. He suggests that lions are social because they are the only big cats that live at high densities, feed on large prey, and live in open habitat. In open habitat a large kill is quickly discovered by vultures and hyenas, and by other lions. Packer hypothesizes that a solitary ancestral lioness feeding on large prey had to defend her kills from other lionesses attracted to the carcass. High lion densities might have meant that the ancestral lioness' mature daughters would have found it difficult to compete for and establish their own home ranges, so it would have made sense for them to remain with her and share kills. The ancestral lioness would still have lost food, but in biological terms it is better to share food with close kin rather than with unrelated lions or other animals.

Of course, Packer's first criterion of high lion density presupposes a high prey density. Bearing that in mind, it is interesting to look at the major differences between lion and tiger habitats. Tigers typically live in forested areas, where visibility is low and where prey are scattered and live at low densities. Because of the dense cover, tigers rarely discover one another's kills and, unlike lions, neighboring tigers rarely compete with one another for carcasses.

One of the few places where tigers live at reasonably high densities in relatively open habitat is Ranthambhore National Park in India. The steep hills of this park are covered with open forest of stunted *dhok* trees. In the dry season most trees are leafless, and both tigers and prey concentrate their activities around water holes. Prey density is not nearly as high as it is in the Serengeti, but Ranthambhore is one of the few places in Asia where the usually solitary, forest-dwelling sambar form large herds.

Unfortunately, there is very little detailed information available on tiger social structure in Ranthambhore, but Fateh Singh, the long-time warden of the park, has identified some tigers by their facial markings. Because the vegetation is so open, he has managed to observe tiger behavior at natural kills, and in 1982 he witnessed an astonishing and significant gathering of tigers. A tigress known as Padmini had killed a Nilgai bull weighing nearly six hundred pounds. While Padmini and her three young cubs fed from the carcass, another adult tigress arrived. It was Lakshmi, Padmini's adult daughter from her first litter. The two adult tigresses scent marked and snarled at each other, but Lakshmi was allowed to feed. As Fateh watched, a third tigress arrived. She was a female known as Nick Ear, Padmini's adult daughter from her second litter. All the tigresses and cubs took turns feeding on the carcass.

Forty-five minutes later, yet another tigress arrived, this one unrelated to Padmini. Then two more tigers, one unidentifiable and the other an adult male, showed up. The male was a littermate of Lakshmi, another offspring of Padmini. All nine tigers fed from the kill in turn, and the observers remarked that Padmini seemed to be in control of the group. While watching the behavior of tigers at bait kills in Chitwan, Chuck McDougal had noticed the same thing; tigers gathering at a bait site deferred to the animal that had actually made the kill and took turns in feeding.

Padmini, her kin, and the others consumed the carcass in twenty-four hours. Had the vegetation been as dense as that in Chitwan, the other tigresses would not have discovered the kill, and Padmini and her three young cubs could probably have fed for three days. However, they shared most of the meat with close kin.

The tigers of Ranthambhore may have given us a fascinating and important glimpse of the evolution of sociality in big cats. Even among normally solitary cats, a large kill made in open habitat quickly attracts neighbors. Perhaps if the habitat were more open and supported a larger number of prey, it would have paid Padmini and her offspring to form a more permanent group to defend their kills against unrelated tigresses. However, this situation probably does not arise very often. Tiger habitat is rarely open, and large prey are not as abundant as they are in the Serengeti. For tigers, living and hunting alone is generally the better option. The advantages of always living in a group to defend the occasional large kill against neighbors do not outweigh the disadvantages of a reduced food intake.

Scattered throughout the old hunting literature are many references to hunters flushing large groups of tigers from kills. People have tended to dismiss these sightings or have suggested that such groups were tigresses accompanied by older cubs. However, the old hunters were probably accurate in their observations. Such groups could easily have been temporary assemblages of related tigresses similar to the group observed by Fateh Singh in Ranthambhore.

Throughout Asia, people are in the process of creating open habitat and high prey densities at reserve boundaries as they remove forest cover and replace it with open fields and herds of domestic animals. Prides of tigers might form under these conditions, but tigers will almost certainly be eradicated from such areas before there is enough time for changes in their solitary ways to evolve.

The theoretically intriguing notion of neighboring tigresses being closely related is also of immediate significance to the tigers' long-term survival. If the pattern observed in Chitwan holds true for tiger populations in general, then all the tigresses in a limited area are likely to be related to some degree. Father-daughter matings, like those that occurred in Chitwan between the Roaring Tigress and the Sauraha Tiger, may be common in small parks and reserves, and this reduced genetic diversity can only hasten the time when the deleterious effects of inbreeding appear. Most human cultures have an incest taboo: parents and offspring, brothers and sisters, first cousins, and close relatives are discouraged by custom or prevented by law from marrying and producing children. Similarly, under normal conditions, animal social systems avoid too many close-relative matings by a natural mechanism known as dispersal, in which young adult animals leave the area where they were born and go off in search of new places to live.

When parks and reserves are small and separated from one another by farmland, villages, or other barriers to migration, animals can neither leave nor enter. As a result, isolated populations develop, and the fate of such populations of animals is nearly always extinction.

The lifespans of the animals concerned, the size of the founding population, and various random events determine how much time a species has before it becomes extinct. Initially, everything looks fine, but then fewer and fewer young survive to breeding age, and females produce fewer offspring. More males than females are born, and relatively rare genes that confer immunity to an occasional disease are lost. In short, it is just a matter of time. Perhaps where tigers are concerned, the Roaring Tigress and her relatives on the floodplain of Chitwan have given us the information we need in time to deal with the problem.

10   A Boat Journey

"**S**AHIB, MEMSAHIB, TEA," said a muffled voice. Kasi Babu crept into our dark, foggy room, breathing through his teeth to emphasize how cold he was. He put down two tepid glasses of tea, and in the weak lantern light went through the elaborate, rather confusing daily ritual of pointing out which glass had sugar in it and which did not. Mel climbed out of bed and peered at the clock.

"What time is it?" I mumbled.

"Quarter to four," he said, "Seems a bit early."

Poor Kasi Babu, I thought, he always seemed to end up with the worst jobs and probably had to get up at least an hour earlier to start a fire and boil a kettle. Still, he would get plenty of sleep while we were away.

It was the start of our boat journey down the Narayani River to Tribinighat, a town on the Indian border. Royal Chitwan National Park had just been officially enlarged, and we wanted to survey the extension for deer and listen for the signal of a radio-collared tiger that had disappeared. The information from the deer survey was important to Dave Smith's study; he was particularly interested in the fate of young, dispersing tigers and wanted to know if outlying areas of the park contained enough prey to support them. We also needed to estimate tiger numbers in the area, and so we had planned a small expedition.

Mel lit a candle, and we groped around for our clothes in the dim light. There is never any hesitation or thought of what to wear when you dress in the cold, predawn darkness, just a mad scramble to put on clothes and warm up. Outside the house the hiccup pump screeched and clanked as Mel washed and I hurried out to join him. The water flowed lukewarm from yesterday's sun-baked ground, steaming in the cold morning air.

From the north came the sounds of people waking up—cocks crowed, babies wailed, and people coughed, hawking and spitting to clear the night devils from their heads. Dogs barked and quarreled, and the clong, clong of buffalo neck bells sounded from the byres as the beasts waited to be milked before they were driven to the stubble fields to graze. On the other side, day noises were taking over from nightjars in the forest. Peacocks honked and miaowed, and a sambar deer belled its deep, resonant alarm call. The sound conjured up the shape of a tiger in the mist and a silent sambar standing cautiously on the river-bank, only its ears twitching for the sound of danger. Slowly the navy-blue sky turned paler blue, then pink. Pinhole stars faded; impercepti-bly, pieces of the Himalayas appeared on the skyline, glowing rose and lavender in the dawn.

We ate breakfast on the run while checking the loaded Jeep. The trailer was packed and unpacked several times in our search for miss-ing items and finally attached to the vehicle. As usual, there were more people traveling than would comfortably fit into the Jeep. Traveling any-where in a motor vehicle in Nepal is like playing the old student game of how many people can squeeze into a telephone booth. The consola-tion in Nepal is that the condition of roads and river crossings is not always reliable, and it is useful to have a large number of people to push.

On this trip there would be nine of us. Dave Smith, the biologist who continued the tiger project after we left, came with his wife-to-be, Francie Cuthbert, an ornithologist. Claude Leyrat, a French veterinarian visiting from Bangkok, and John Poppleton, a young field assistant working for Dave, were joined by three *shikaris*: Vishnu Tamang, the cook, tracker, and jack-of-all-trades; Hit Bahadur, the slightly deaf, one-time royal *shikari*; and Bul Bahadur, the veteran, reputed to be able to carry a hundred pounds on his back all day. In addition to Mel and me, there was also a rather handsome black-and-white goat, which we in-tended to eat. We planned to drive to the river confluence near Tiger Tops where we had arranged to meet the boats, and then float down-stream through the park to the Indian border. There were no roads in this part of the park, so Kancha Lama would drive a long, circui-tous route, rendezvousing with us at Tribinighat so we could all return in the Jeep.

The vehicle was very full, and when we were finally underway there was an ominous cracking noise from beneath it every time we went over a bump. I asked Vishnu about the noise. "Okay, okay," he as-sured me. "Very strong Jeep."

We descended the steep bank at the bullock-cart ford to the Rapti River. As we reached the water's edge, Kancha Lama leaped from his seat on the roof, opened the hood, and tied a plastic bag around the distributor, smiling in approval at his own foresight. He also tied a small bunch of marigolds to the radiator. "For good luck," he explained. We crept forward into the two-foot-deep water, Dave driving while Kancha Lama and Hit Bahadur gave directions from the roof: "Left . . . left . . . straight . . . straight! No, left . . . okay! Okay!" Because Kancha Lama had once guided us into a deep hole in this authoritative fashion, we did not rely completely upon his instructions.

Once we crossed the river and reached the park road, Dave and Mel moved to the hood of the Jeep while Kancha Lama drove. There was a chance we might pick up some data in the form of tiger tracks. Sitting next to Kancha Lama, my view was almost completely obscured by Mel and Dave, and as we clattered across the first of twenty or so rickety wooden bridges, I hoped he could see more than I could. Then Mel put his hand on the windscreen behind him, a signal to stop, and at that instant there was a blood-curdling roar from the road ahead. The figures on the hood sat rock still, and I peered through the gap between them at the impressive figure of a female sloth bear twenty feet in front of us.

In the filtered sunlight her long, coarse, black fur stood out in crisp detail, and the white V-shaped marking on her throat flashed as she alternately stood on her hind feet in a threat gesture and dropped to all fours, unable to decide whether to charge us or run. Behind her, two shaggy, spaniel-sized bundles of fur tried to climb onto her back every time she dropped to the ground. At the fourth attempt they made it, and their mother carried them off into the forest, pausing to look over her shoulder to make sure we were not following. The cubs clung to her back precariously, grasping wedges of her long fur between their teeth and clinging on with all four feet.

One of the most dangerous animals in Chitwan, the sloth bear ranks second after the rhino on the dubious honors list of animals that kill or injure the most people each year. Tigers and leopards are much less of a threat, for they generally go out of their way to avoid humans. Sloth bears are short-sighted, unpredictable, and often attack when encountered at close range. The bear's rather odd name is thought to date back to the late 1700s, when a shaggy skin was first identified as that of a sloth. The animal was subsequently classified as a true bear, but the "sloth" part of the name remained. Adult males may weigh up to three hundred pounds; for creatures so large, they have a very unusual diet consisting mainly of ants and termites. Large, protruding lips, a mobile snout, nostrils that can be tightly closed, and a hollow palate enable them to suck up termites like a vacuum cleaner. We often heard their strange huffing and blowing before we saw them, head and shoulders deep in the remains of a termite mound. Their long, powerful claws that are so effective at ripping open the rock-hard mounds also can do considerable damage to a person, and their habit of standing on their hind feet when alarmed usually results in people being mauled around the face and chest.

For the next few miles after our encounter with the sloth bears, the two-rut road cut a narrow swath through one of the largest expanses of tall grass in the park. We felt like crickets in a hayfield. The tall, feathery-topped stems were twenty-five feet high in places, and the wall of blades was punctuated by tunnels. The larger gaps were marked with rhino scrapes, two parallel scars in the soil made by males as they drag their hind feet while urine marking. Ahead on the grassy strip in the center of the road, something gray and fluffy, like rabbit fur, moved in the breeze. We stopped to look. It was a dried-out tiger scat, weathered down to just the hair of whatever had been eaten. Mel collected it and passed it back into the cab for safekeeping; we would analyze it later.

At the edge of this sea of grass, there was a hut by a small stream, and a red-and-white barrier across the road. The lonely sound of someone playing a drum came from the hut, but there was no one in sight. We stopped and waited. This was Dumaria *chowki*, a checkpoint staffed by army guards. Some five hundred armed troops of the Royal Nepal Army guard the park at two dozen of these isolated outposts. Their job is to discourage poachers and maintain a log of the occasional vehicles that travel the road. The drum stopped, and a uniformed guard dashed out with a book for us to sign. He was followed by another guard bent double under the weight of a small tin trunk and a bedroll. He, it transpired, was being posted to another checkpoint and needed a lift. According to the log book, the last vehicle to pass this way had come ten days ago, so despite our already bulging load we told him to throw his baggage in the trailer and climb on the roof.

The Reu River is a smaller, prettier version of the main Rapti and flows diagonally across the park. It eventually joins the larger Rapti River but must be forded just in front of Tiger Tops Jungle Lodge. The well-used crossing looked still and shallow by comparison to the wide, swift Rapti we had crossed earlier that morning, so after a brief inspection of the ford, we drove in with confidence. The nose of the Jeep plunged into a shallow hole and stuck, much to the entertainment of a group of birdwatchers and several hotel staff members.

Wading around the vehicle, we discovered that water depth was not the problem; we had hit a patch of quicksand and the trailer was sinking fast. Kancha Lama tried to restart the engine while everyone else pushed and gave directions. The Jeep eventually came free with a

Stuck at the Reu River crossing.

squelching roar, showering us with mud and water. As we stood in the river watching Jeep and trailer stagger up the opposite bank, a party of tourists in a Tiger Tops Land Rover whizzed by through the correct crossing, not ten feet from our sticking place.

At the lodge we confirmed our arrangements to rent boats and stopped to talk with Chuck and Margie McDougal. Chuck looked harassed. He had planned to come with us on the river trip, but a plane due to take thirty guests back to Kathmandu had failed to arrive and had left him with a full house. He was forced to bow out, but he sent us on our way with a generous gift of beer, and we left to rendezvous with the boats.

Just west of Tiger Tops, the Reu and Rapti Rivers join and flow into the larger Narayani River, which continues west for a while and then turns south to the Indian border, eventually joining the Ganges River. The confluence of the Reu, Rapti, and Narayani rivers is a jumbled, desolate place. Vast expanses of sand, pebbles, and boulders are strewn with uprooted trees left by the monsoon floods. Splintered and broken, their roots stripped clean, the trees are a testament to the power of the river and the magnitude of the erosion problem in the hills from which the rivers flow.

From the mess of roots and branches, chestnut-headed bee-eaters whirred and looped in diminutive aerial ballets, snapping insects out of the air and returning to beat them furiously against their perches. In the river, rows of cormorants stood shoulder to shoulder on an invisible sandbar like a crowd of orderly passengers on a sinking

The confluence of the Reu, Rapti, and Narayani rivers after the monsoon rains.

ship. As we drove toward the lump of palm fronds that was the boat-men's hut, three black-necked storks that had been marching purpose-fully up and down the shoreline took to the air.

There were two boats, each of which was manned by two *bhotes*, (pronounced bo-tay), members of a tribe of fishermen and river people indigenous to the *terai*. Traditionally the *bhotes* have made their living from the river, building small, temporary camps on the bank and bar-tering fish for rice with villagers, but with the influx of tourists some now rent out their boats and river knowledge to the new hotels.

Close to shore, where the shallow water was translucent green above the rounded pebbles, each *bhote* propelled his boat by paddling with one spadelike foot, weight on the other knee inside the boat as if he were pushing a scooter. The *bhotes'* broad, triangular feet were soled with half-inch-thick calluses from years of foot paddling. However, we were going downstream, and as soon as we reached deeper water they used fifteen-foot sticks as punting poles. We drifted gently in the cur-rent, with just an occasional guiding push. As if by mutual consent, everyone was quiet: the water whispering against the side of the boat and the occasional thump of the pole were only small sounds against the rush of the river.

There were birds everywhere, as if we had suddenly floated into a real-life museum diorama. Tight-knit flights of teal circled, inspecting us. Black ibis probed sand patches on the bank, and pairs of coppery-gold Brahiminy ducks dotted every sandbar, aw-aw-awing in mild alarm as we drifted near. Kingfishers, river terns, and unidentifiable waders surrounded us, then a crested serpent eagle screamed at us from a tree on the bank, not ten feet above our heads.

Moving at the river's pace, we slid by a sandbar where five slim, gray-green shapes lay motionless in the sun. They were gharial, the rare, fish-eating crocodiles. Their large eyes and slender snouts edged with dozens of small, sharp teeth give them a delicate, primitive air, and they seemed quicker and more gracile than the rest of the croco-dile clan as they vanished into the water in a silent swirl. There were only about fifty gharial left in the entire Narayani river system, and we were seeing part of the largest wild population in existence. Of the fifty, only seven were males, but there were none in the group we had just seen. Mature males have a strange protruberance on the tips of their snouts known as a *ghara*, which means "pitcher" in Hindi. The *ghara* has been one the causes of the gharial's decline, for the males are sought and killed by local people who believe the *ghara* has various mystical powers, including aphrodisiacal properties and the ability to keep fields fertile for seven years.

As noon approached, the air trembled with heat, merging with the ripples on the river to form a single shimmering surface. We sat silently in the boat beneath large black umbrellas, like relics of the *raj*, while the *bhotes* occasionally stirred the water with their poles. A small flotilla of green-and-black dragonflies trailed each boat, snapping at invisible insects, and except for the endlessly repeated "Koo-koo-karoooo" of spotted wood doves, even the birds were stifled into silence.

To our right, tall, white egrets stalked along the shoreline of an oxbow recently deserted by the main stream. During hot weather, tigers frequently spend the day near water, so the oxbow was a good place to search for tracks. We guided the boats into the quiet backwater and walked off in different directions to speed the search. The ground was studded with deep, intimidating footprints of rhino that seemed to multiply as I walked farther away from the boat and the safety of num-bers. Soft sand turned to pebbles and boulders, and I realized I had forgotten my sandals, so I headed toward the old, collapsed riverbank for easier walking. Selecting the path of least resistance, I forgot about the rhinos and was delighted to find that a tigress had walked this route the night before—perhaps the rocks had hurt her feet too. Every path through the crumbled ridge was beaten flat by chital hooves; more likely the tigress had been using the bank for cover to ambush deer coming down to drink.

On the Narayani River, passing through the Siwalik Hills. Our party, from the back of the boat: the bhote, Hit Bahadur and Claude, Fiona and Mel, and Francie.

Sending Vishnu and the equipment boat on ahead to the next river intersection to start lunch, we photographed and measured the tracks for future reference, then continued to search for signs of other wildlife. There were tracks of jackal, jungle cat, fishing cat, and otter as well as deer, and the humanlike footprint of a sloth bear. There was also a crossing for domestic buffalo, where village boys had swum their herds across the river to graze in the lush pastures of the park. Even in this remote and inaccessible place, there seemed to be no sure way of protecting the park from the impact of people and their livestock.

Hot, hungry, and vaguely discouraged, we returned to the boat to set off in search of the next side stream and, we hoped, Vishnu. We found him cooking rice in the midst of a jumble of boulders. With the goat feeding on the pile of leaves beside him, he looked like a rather well-equipped castaway on a desert island. Although lunch was only rice and *dhal* (boiled lentils), we ate fast and hungrily, Nepali style, with our fingers. As we ate, a tiny, wrinkled man in a loincloth, carrying a load of bamboo on his head, trotted out of the park forest behind us. "Namaste," he said, and with this single word of greeting disappeared along the bank of the main river. "Another hunter-gatherer trying to make a living," said Claude. "Yes," said Mel, "except he's probably going to sell it in the market rather than use it himself."

In many parts of the world, the problems of hunter-gatherer people versus parks and preserves have grown more severe as pressures on protected areas increase. Both parks and people have their champions, but no one has yet been able to suggest solutions equally good for both.

142

Hunter-gatherers traditionally have lived at low densities. Many of them originally were nomadic peoples who harvested everything they needed from the forest and small plots of cultivated land. They traded among themselves, but there were not enough people to make a serious impact on the environment. Today, they harvest forest products like bamboo, fruits, nuts, and wood to sell in the open market, and demand is not limited to their own needs or those of their immediate neighbors. Trying to satisfy the requirements of a much wider market, they put a greater strain on the ecosystem, and many park authorities have had no option but to resettle people and attempt to convince them to exchange their traditional ways for those of settled farmers. Critics of this resettlement policy maintain that primitive tribes are as much a part of the ecosystem as the wildlife and in need of the same degree of protection. However, for the authorities, protection of a people's way of life is much more complex and difficult than trying to protect wildlife and poses a variety of ethical and practical dilemmas.

As we cleared away the scanty remains of lunch, Vishnu cheered everybody up with an unlikely story about being chased down the river by a monster crocodile that he said was after the goat. Pantomiming wildly, he waved his arms in a plausible imitation of crocodile jaws but spoiled the effect by making tiger roars to show how fierce it had been. Back in the boat, looking for crocodiles, we pointed out logs and likely flurries of water to Vishnu, asking jokingly, "Was that it?" until a sudden burst of spray startled everyone.

Two river dolphins appeared, jumping and blowing beside the boat, so close we could almost touch them. There were pinkish gray, with domed foreheads and tiny, pea-sized eyes. Because they seemed so tame, Dave and John decided to swim with the dolphins and plunged into the swift water. The river had narrowed and was flowing fast and milky-green through a steep-sided gorge. The water smelled deep and cold, and John and Dave could barely keep up with the boat, let alone the dolphins. They swam for a while, the sound of splashing echoing off the rocky walls above the roar of the river; once back on board they shivered uncontrollably, even in the warm sun.

The sides of the gorge rose steeper and higher, and the river grew narrower and more turbulent. Folded, uplifted cliffs of white limestone ran beside us, the clear lines of sedimentation undulating like waves. We were floating through part of the fossil-rich Siwalik Hills, and it would have been fun to stop and explore, but we had to push on to reach a campsite before dark.

As the sun sank toward the horizon, the light changed from the white heat of midday to a liquid gold brilliance—Kodachrome light, where shadows outlined every detail, exaggerating dimensions. The turning leaves of the sal trees were lit like colored lanterns, and shadows gave back to the forest a depth unnoticed in the flat light of midday.

If it had not been for the *bhotes'* intimate knowledge of the river, we would have missed our campsite in the dark. It was seven o'clock when we beached the boats by starlight and carried our equipment to a broad, sandy spot one hundred yards from the water. While we pitched the tent in a black cave of trees, the *shikaris* scraped together enough wood for a small cooking fire. Because this was a traditional *bhote* campsite, there was very little firewood around, and so everyone wandered off with dim flashlights to try and find enough to last for the evening.

We ate rice, lentils, and curried potatoes while waving furiously at clouds of delighted mosquitoes and afterward hurriedly organized the sleeping arrangements. We had a six-man tent and a fly sheet, both ancient relics of a mountain expedition that we had bought at bargain prices in the Kathmandu bazaar. The *shikaris* said they preferred to sleep under the fly sheet in bedrolls, and Claude insisted he never slept in tents, so that left five of us. While Claude fumbled around in the bushes trying to string up his mosquito net, the rest of us moved some of the more perishable goods into the tent, amazed that six people were supposed to fit into it.

Around midnight I was awakened by the goat bleating and Claude shouting about a leopard. Mel stuck his head out of the tent to inquire what the noise was all about. "It must be a leopard," Claude insisted. "Listen to the goat." Mel was unsympathetic. "You're much too large to be a prey item," he told Claude. Nevertheless, he climbed out of the tent, stoked the fire, and gave the now-quiet goat something to eat.

An hour later Claude woke us all again. "Fire!" he bellowed. "There's a huge fire coming toward us!" Sure enough, the entire hillside above us was ablaze, filling the air with smoke. Dave asked Vishnu and Hit Bahadur if they'd seen a fire when they were gathering wood. After much discussion, it transpired that the *shikaris* had indeed seen a fire— in fact, they had lit it. Vishnu explained that at the time the wind had been blowing the other way; they had set the fire because they wanted to be able to see to collect wood. "Good grief, what terrible reasoning," Mel groaned. "For heaven's sake get up there and put it out or cut a firebreak or something."

Vishnu, Hit Bahadur, and Bul Bahadur set off unwillingly in the direction of the fire, while Mel and Dave went back to bed. I watched the glowing line change direction and veer away from us. The flames were only a few inches high and moving slowly through the fallen sal leaves, clearing the ground and not doing much damage. The damp night air would probably extinguish the fire before daybreak. Scrambling back down the hill, Vishnu announced, "Fire gone out, gone the other way," and disappeared promptly into his bedroll. I sat for a while listening to the tumultuous chorus of frogs. Their individual songs merged into one continuous roar, overlaid by the nightjars' steady "Chunk, chunk, chunk," like someone methodically chopping wood.

The *shikaris* woke us at five in the morning. It was cold, and we all dressed in as many articles of clothing as we had brought. It seemed strange that in three or four hours we would all be hot, but the thought made us relish the chill with a kind of perverse satisfaction. I walked down to the stream to wash and along the edge of the water found fresh leopard tracks. Everyone was strung out along the stream at intervals, brushing their teeth, and we all seemed to notice the tracks at the same time. "There *was* a leopard!" yelled Claude triumphantly. "I could have been killed!" We followed the tracks up the streambed until they disappeared into the forest some twenty yards behind our tent. Mel and Dave agreed it would be wise to eat the goat that night, before the leopard decided it was too tempting.

Conversation at breakfast revolved around the day's hike up the stream and what we ought to wear on our feet. The plan was to walk some five miles up the tributary and look for tiger tracks on the way. We also wanted to assess the number of prey, so at several places we would angle off into the forest along a compass line and run a transect or sample strip. Every hundred yards along the line, we would stop and identify all the animal droppings in a measured area. Dave hoped this information would provide an index of prey density that he could compare with data from other forests. This information about prey might provide national park managers with a quick and easy way to predict the areas that would be good for tigers.

Our seemingly mundane discussion of footwear was in fact crucial, since whatever we chose would have to stand up to wading, sharp rocks, steep hills, thorns, and spiky palms. Most of us settled for tennis shoes except Claude, who wore a smart pair of brown suede boots, and the two *bhotes*, who wore bare feet for everything.

We set off up the tributary at seven, leaving Vishnu and the two other *bhotes* to deal with the goat. Before we left there had been a brief argument about the animal's fate, but I was the only person in favor of keeping it alive. Around us, hidden in the mist, unidentifiable birds sang a strange, melancholy series of unrelated notes. We never saw the

Counting pellets and measuring vegetation density along a transect line.

bird that sang this haunting early morning symphony. Francie thought it might be a *Leiothrix*, and the *bhotes* said the sounds came from spirits. Both explanations seemed equally plausible in the dripping gray fog.

Crossing and recrossing the shallow stream that was studded with slippery rocks, the *bhotes* were in their element. The rest of us, struggling to keep our feet dry, made slower progress. A barking deer, surprised at his morning drink, scuttled up the steep bank like a rabbit, the dry rattle of fallen sal leaves marking the direction of his flight. A troop of hanuman langurs uttered their "Kok-kok-kok" alarm call but stayed to watch us go by. It was a large group of about twenty-five adults, and four of the females held tiny, wizened babies. As if he thought we might consider him a negligent troop leader, the big male jumped up and down and made the branches sway when we came too close.

The mist dissipated, and the air filled with the sounds of other birds: doves, bulbuls, mynas, and babblers. Sharp cries of parakeets bounced and echoed off the steep, rocky walls, following us as we splashed on up the stream. We found fresh tracks of a tigress and one large cub and followed them along the riverbed for some time, losing them periodically among the rocks but always picking them up again. The sun came out, and everyone began to shed layers of clothing.

The right bank of the stream became steeper, until eventually it was a rocky cliff a hundred and fifty feet high. Mosses, liverworts, and ferns hung from the shaded fissures, and small, gray-blue rock thrushes pecked and hopped among the wet rock crevices. The other side of the river was a sandbank, stirred and crisscrossed by the heart-shaped hooves of wild bison or gaur, at least twenty of them judging by their tracks.

Further on, where the streambed divided, we left the comparatively easy walking of the river and headed into the hilly forest. Stunted sal trees clung to the dry, rocky slopes, and the broken canopy let the sunlight through to a dense understory of head-high grass, bushes, and palm trees. Every hundred yards we carefully raked away the leaves from a measured circle of ground and counted and identified all the animal droppings. We measured the density of the vegetation and recorded such signs of human activity as wood cutting or cattle grazing.

Later, when Dave Smith analyzed the data, he found that prey density was a good predictor of the way tigers used an area. Sites with a low index of prey abundance were used only temporarily or merely traveled through, whereas areas with a high prey density were used year round; tigers chose such areas as home ranges and became permanent residents. In most cases, vegetation density was also a good predictor and seemed to be closely tied to prey density. Where there was little ground vegetation, there were few prey animals, and tigers were less likely to use the area. The transect results did not produce any major surprises and basically confirmed what we already knew. However, we did show that instead of walking through an area and saying, "Mmm, this looks pretty good for tigers," it was possible to create a standardized indexing method that could be used quickly and easily in many different types of forests.

Tired and hungry, we headed back to camp in the early evening. Everyone was walking fast, almost at a trot, and coming back down the riverbed I was behind Bul Bahadur, the old *shikari*. I followed him, watching where he put his feet and where he jumped, falling in with his half walk–half run rhythm. I was in an exhausted daze, but it was easy, automatic; I felt as if I could walk another twenty miles. On such walks I was usually at the end of the line, slow and hesitant in deciding what rock to leap to next and whether I should wade a section of stream or try to jump it. But in following Bul Bahadur I discovered the secret of efficient travel in that kind of terrain: he built up momentum, then let it

Arriving in Tribinighat.

carry him, never allowing his feet to pause long in any one place. He skimmed the unstable river rocks, resting his weight on each one for such a short time that it never had a chance to tip or roll; if it did, he was already gone. It was like following a dancer.

Next morning we broke camp, packed the boats, and set off for the Nepal-India border. The steep hills flattened, and the river slowed and broadened into a lake just before the dam at Tribinighat. Houses, tea shops, and temples lined the shore, and wisps of blue smoke rose from cremations at the burning *ghats* on the north bank. Ignoring the evidence and all advice, John filled his water bottle from the lake.

A broad, stone stairway led up from the water to the center of town. The Jeep was parked at the top of the stairs, and beside it stood Kancha Lama, an inveterate womanizer, engrossed in explaining something to a group of giggling girls. He shooed them away sheepishly when he saw us. We tied up the boats and went in search of a tea shop. The town was a tired, worn-out-looking place. Long-legged chickens strode knowledgeably about the dusty streets, fighting for scraps in stinking heaps of garbage. The tea shops were marked by clusters of emaciated dogs that stood still as Giacometti sculptures, waiting for handouts. We ordered tea all round and three packets of biscuits and tried surreptitiously to feed the dogs, but a bent, toothless old woman drove them off with an accurate volley of stones.

After tea, we walked across the dam and watched a thin veil of water spilling over the concrete barrier. Old men and small boys lined the railing, watching the falling water intently. Below them in the spray hung rows of flat, woven baskets of various shapes and sizes, some built around old umbrella frames set to catch the inch-long, flashing fish fry that were being swept over the dam. In Nepal, almost all the protein in the average person's diet comes from lentils and pulses. For most people, the price of a chicken is more than a week's wages, so fish, no matter what size, is much sought after, especially as it can often be acquired by a simple investment of time on the part of small boys and old men.

That afternoon we crossed to the other side of the lake and walked up a side stream to run some more transects. The water was brown and soapy with scum from a brewery, a collection of huts surrounded by

Dave and Francie in a Tribinighat tea shop.

Pedestal erosion outside the park.

A young village girl tending cattle.

evil-smelling drums and tubs of fermenting liquid. On the other side of the stream lay a piece of forest that looked fairly undisturbed. Dave walked out onto the white sand to check for radio signals from the missing tiger. As he stood with earphones on, pointing the antenna toward the trees, a soldier appeared with a rifle and shouted at him to go back. Inadvertently, Dave had stepped across the border into India.

Traveling back to Tiger Tops in the Jeep, we paralleled the river we had just floated down, only now we were outside the park. We saw a vivid illustration of the power that one hundred thousand people have to alter the landscape. Twenty years ago or so, the area had been virgin sal forest and grassland. Now fields and clusters of houses stretched all the way to the outline of the Mahabharat Hills. Almost uninhabited a quarter of a century ago, this part of the *terai* had now become one of the most heavily populated areas in Nepal. Only hacked-over remains of a few giant simal trees rose above fields that once had been tall grasslands, and patches of scrubby sal trees stood on orange-pink pedestals of earth, textbook examples of erosion following deforestation.

Forest areas outside the park are being rapidly converted to farmland.

Historical accounts and scientific data agree that the tall grass and riverine forest habitats of the *dun* valley floodplains support an extraordinarily large animal biomass. In Chitwan the biomass, or weight of animals in a given area, is the second highest in Asia and approaches the figures from some of the East African national parks. Unfortunately, very little floodplain habitat outside the park remains uncultivated, and the animal biomass estimates from sal forest, the predominant vegetation type both inside and outside the park, are much lower. When sal forest is subjected to intense grazing and wood collecting, the herbaceous understory either disappears or is replaced by un-palatable aromatic weeds. These changes make the forest all but use-less to deer, other wildlife, or even domestic stock.

The vivid contrast between the forest inside the park and the area we were driving through was a sad reminder of how Chitwan was being girdled by the combined pressures of agriculture, grazing, and wood-cutting. Empty, dwindling patches of forest and intensively farmed land border the long northern boundary of the park, while multiple-use for-est lands extend east and west for a short distance until roads, forests, and agriculture commence again. Although the new park extension contained a healthy deer population and we had found plenty of tiger sign, it was obvious that Chitwan was becoming an island.

11   *Luxury in the Jungle*

*O*N OUR WAY BACK from Tribinighat after our survey of the western end of the park, we returned to Tiger Tops Jungle Lodge, where Chuck McDougal would be interested to hear our impressions of the new park addition. Besides, after days of only hot tea and lukewarm water, the thought of an icy, cold drink had assumed enormous importance.

However we were not an impressive sight. Days of camping and sitting on the sand had taken its toll on our clothes, and we were unaware of quite how dirty we were. The Jeep was overfull, the muffler had fallen off, and the vehicle was making a noise like a tank. Two *shikaris* sat on the roof and another sat on the hood. There were eight people inside, smothered under backpacks, radio-tracking equipment, jerricans, and other camping paraphernalia. As we roared slowly into the driveway of the lodge, I felt a twinge of doubt about our appearance but pushed it aside with visions of cold beer and gleaming porcelain toilets.

Tiger Tops is a luxurious and expensive hotel that caters for tourists who want to see wildlife in style. A night there costs as much as a Nepali government worker earns in a month, so the guests are an eclectic assortment of other nationalities, predominantly European and American. Guests fly from Kathmandu to Chitwan in a specially chartered plane and travel from the grass airstrip to the lodge aboard a line of elephants. Although Tiger Tops has no electricity, ice and fresh produce are flown in daily, and one can have a hot shower (courtesy of solar panels), a fine meal, or a cold drink.

The main portion of the lodge is a large, circular stone building topped with a thatch roof it houses the dining room, bar, and gathering place and fits quietly and beautifully into the jungle setting. Built in the early 1960s by John Coapman, the lodge is modeled on some of the East African luxury hotels. Jim Edwards and Chuck McDougal, who have owned and run the place since the mid-1970s, have deliberately resisted expansion, and the main lodge sleeps only forty guests. There is also a less luxurious tented camp on one of the islands in the Narayani River.

A few visitors sipping tea in the tranquil shade of the verandah watched quietly as we uncoiled ourselves from our battered vehicle, pounded clouds of dust from our clothes, and headed for the amenities.

The bathroom was cool and dim, its walls lined with gleaming white tiles. Piles of fat, fresh towels and bars of scented soap lay on a table near the basin, and I washed my face, arms, and hands slowly, savoring the hot water. Glaring at my dust-caked hair in the mirror, I noticed a handsome, shiny-green hairclip posed elegantly on one side of my head. I couldn't remember owning such a thing, much less wearing it on a camping trip, so I investigated. As it began to struggle, I discovered it was a huge, iridescent beetle.

Everyone else had started on second beers by the time I rejoined them, and the talk as usual was of the movements and activities of tigers in the area. Chuck had arrived and was filling us in on the tigers that had been to his bait sites, who had cubs, and who was scent marking where. Mel and Dave added bits of information about the radio-collared animals, and we all speculated about what might be going on. Astonishingly hospitable as usual, Chuck invited us to dinner and offered us beds for the night so we could continue the discussion. We accepted immediately.

The dining room was filling up with freshly showered guests who had dressed for dinner—men in safari suits or neatly pressed jeans, women looking studiedly casual with deliberately confused hair. Several woman wore long dresses and high heels. One corner of the room that was given over to a library and small museum of bones and skulls was occupied by a group of Japanese men, exclaiming over a rhino tooth. No one seemed too offended by our dusty presence, and the smartly uniformed bearer handing round *hors d'oeuvres* only smiled when we took handfuls of cheese balls. After our miles of walking, we were all starving.

At dinner we sat with Chuck, an elderly, calm couple from Boston, and a British "average adjuster" from Singapore. Chuck told us of the tremendous run of luck they'd had at the tented camp: a tigress had been bringing her three large cubs in to the bait site regularly for nearly a month.

For the past six years Chuck had kept meticulous records of every tiger that visited each of the Lodge's bait sites. Most of the tigers could be identified by their distinctive facial markings, or sometimes from their tracks alone. While going through his records, Chuck had discovered that there were distinct differences in the ways tigers of different sexes and ages made use of bait sites.

Young male tigers were the most frequent visitors at Chuck's bait sites. They showed up two and a half times more often than would have been expected from their percentage in the population. The next most frequent visitors were tigresses with large cubs more than a year old. Adult males were third on the list, and after them, as we had suspected, were tigresses with young cubs less than a year old. Surprisingly, at the bottom of the list were young females, who came to bait sites even less often than the ultracautious tigresses with small cubs.

It was intriguing that young males headed the list, while their sisters rarely used the bait sites. Chuck thought this difference reflected the strategies of the two sexes. He argued that because of the home-range pattern, in which one male has exclusive access to several females, and because of the sex ratio in the adult population of three females to one male, competition between males was going to be intense. Therefore bold, enterprising behavior was probably a very good strategy. Males use bait sites more when they are becoming adults, a vulnerable, transitional stage. When they mature and manage to establish a territory, they cannot afford to stay in one place too long, otherwise another male will take over the unvisited portions of their range. Females, on the other hand, ensure the survival of their cubs by maintaining a low profile, keeping away from potentially harmful encounters with other tigers. However, when the cubs are larger and less vulnerable, the attraction of an easy meal may outweigh the possible dangers of a bait site.

Our conversation was interrupted by a *shikari*, who padded softly into the dining room and whispered something into Chuck's ear. Chuck put his napkin on the table and rose to his feet. "Quiet, please," he said. "Ladies and gentlemen, the tiger has killed." A murmur of excitement went round the room. "Anyone who would like to see the tiger at the bait kill, please follow me. Your dinners will be kept warm for you." All over the dining hall, chairs squeaked against the stone floor as people stood up. This was the moment they had all been waiting for, but now that it had arrived many of them seemed not quite sure if they wanted to go or not.

Finally a group of about twenty collected at the door, ourselves included. Although we had seen many tigers, we were not about to pass up the chance to see another one. "No cameras, please. It will be too dark for photographs," instructed Chuck. "Please don't talk, and be prepared to take your shoes off when I ask you to."

With the *shikari* noiselessly leading the way, we walked quietly out into the dark, stumbling slightly after the bright lights of the dining room. The sounds of the forest were loud around us; people muttered worriedly, out of their element and nervous of the night. In front of me, three Japanese men smelling of Lux soap walked swiftly with the small steps of practised hikers. One of them had a miner's lamp attached to the front of his peaked baseball cap, and as he switched it on the brilliant white beam stabbed at the dark trees.

"Turn that light off!" Chuck snapped, but before his words could be translated the offender stumbled and fell, and the bright beam lurched skywards and went out. Bumping into each other, everyone stopped, but his companions quickly hustled their baseball-capped friend to his feet and we were off again. After we had walked for ten minutes, our eyes became accustomed to the starlight. We stopped in a small huddle at a junction of trails, where Chuck was shining a dim torch along a smooth path that led up a *nullah*.

"I'd like everyone to take their shoes off here," he said quietly. "You can see that the path has been swept clean, so you don't have to worry about treading on anything. Walk slowly, in single file, and don't make any noise. The blind is about two hundred yards away." A well-dressed woman in a long skirt and nylons started to protest but changed her mind and left her shoes in a pile with everyone else's. We walked silently along the trail, feeling the fine, cool dust between our toes. A sliver of moon cast barely visible shadows on the path, and only the sound of collective breathing and clothes rustling marked our passage.

A hundred yards from the shoe pile I heard a noise like someone crunching on a stick of celery. The sound grew louder as we walked until it reached the same volume as the scratchy chorus of frogs. I suddenly realized I had heard that sound before and recognized what it was. The tiger was chewing on a bone. We reached the blind, a twenty-foot-long grass structure, and filed inside. Everyone lined up along the row of peepholes facing the *nullah*, and Chuck slowly turned up the spotlight positioned above the bait.

There he was, a young male tiger, up to his elbows in buffalo. The spotlight and the foliage had the effect of making the scene look faintly improbable, like a painting on black velvet. He was on the other side of the *nullah*, fifty feet away at our eye level. It was as if he was on stage and knew it. He turned his great head toward us and looked for a long time, then went back to his meal. Exquisite, dark gold, and gleaming, he was somehow more impressive for being seen at night.

The crunching noise went on and on—no wonder there is hardly anything left at the site of a kill, I thought. But then, as if he had played out his part, he rose swiftly to his feet, gave us one long, intense look, and moved off quickly into the darkness, disappearing the instant he stepped out of the circle of light. Everyone took a deep breath.

"Don't make any noise," Chuck whispered. "He's probably just waiting until we leave so he can finish his meal." He turned off the spotlight and we trod quietly down the path toward the road. I wondered if the Tiger Tops guests knew how lucky they were. So few people ever see a tiger outside a zoo or a circus. Those who are privileged to see a tiger in the wild must come away with the certain knowledge that, whatever it costs, it is worth preserving this great cat in its natural setting.

Later, back at Chuck's house near the Lodge, the conversation turned again to biology. Those not as involved as we were must have thought our discussions long and tedious, filled with minute details of no possible value or interest. What did it matter in the grand scheme of things where the Sauraha Tiger was on any given day? But for us, a brief encounter or an unusual move were clues—like trying to solve a crime, there was excitement in discovering a pattern or seeing a prediction fulfilled. We tossed guesses as to what might be going on or what might happen next back and forth, rejecting possibilities or incorporating bits of information into new theories. Surely, this is one of the major forces that drives any scientist—the pure excitement of discovery, the heightened energy and thrill of pursuing an idea.

Provoked by Chuck's data and fueled by a bottle of rum, talk turned to the different strategies of male and female tigers. It was clear that tigresses competed among themselves for rights to a home range that had the essentials for raising cubs. They came to know these areas well, reusing rest sites, denning places, and good hunting areas in a far more fine-grained fashion than males and generally maintaining the same territory for years. Two of the tigresses Chuck was monitoring had been residents for ten years or more.

A tigress' "biological success" is measured in the number of her cubs that reach adulthood. However, unlike a male, a tigress bears the responsibility of keeping cubs fed and teaching them the complicated business of fending for themselves. Cubs continue to suckle until they are four or five months old, but even after they are weaned, they initially lack the ability or skill to kill for themselves. Not only do cubs have to learn the complex skills of finding and stalking prey, but until they are about a year old they lack the permanent canine teeth needed to dispatch prey efficiently. These large, daggerlike teeth are essential for delivering the killing bite to large prey and also are important instruments in opening up a carcass. Prem, our chief *shikari*, once tied out a small goat for some orphaned cubs that were about six months old. When he returned to the site the next day, he found that the cubs had somehow managed to kill the goat, but the carcass was intact. It had been licked clean of hair, and there were small tooth marks all over it. The milk teeth of the cubs had been unable to penetrate the goat's skin.

Even when the cubs are a year old, they still are not capable of killing for themselves, and with two or three hungry mouths to feed the tigress has to step up her hunting rate significantly. This is the time when normally ultracautious females are attracted to the relatively easy pickings of baits. Young tigers learn to kill for themselves by imitation and practice, and their mother provides them with opportunities to test their skills. Most observations of cubs learning to tackle large prey have been made at bait sites, but there is no reason to doubt that they practice in the same way on natural kills when the opportunity arises.

Partly because they lack their permanent canines, but also because of inexperience, even quite large cubs are often unable to kill a tethered buffalo or large deer. They bite and claw the unfortunate beast, sometimes managing to pull it down, but they don't seem quite sure where or how the killing bite should be delivered. In his book *The Deer and the Tiger*, George Schaller vividly describes a scene he witnessed in Kanha National Park in India, when a tigress seemed to be teaching her three twelve-month-old cubs how to kill. As he watched at a bait site, a buffalo kept the three cubs at bay for two and a half hours. When the tigress arrived, she grabbed the buffalo by the hind leg and threw it to the ground. The cubs leaped onto it, biting and clawing at random while the tigress released her grip and stepped back. The buffalo shook the cubs off and struggled to its feet with only superficial wounds. The cubs tried again, with the same lack of success, until the tigress threw the buffalo to the ground with the same technique she had used earlier. Once again the cubs swarmed all over the buffalo, biting and clawing, but as soon as the tigress released her hold, the buffalo once again rose to its feet. The cubs finally made the kill, but it had been a long struggle.

A tigress is responsible for feeding and protecting her cubs through this two-year period of trial and error. When they are older, cubs may wander off for days at a time to test their skills, but they rejoin their mother for a meal if they are unsuccessful in the hunt. Cubs are very vulnerable when they are small and left alone at the den site, not only to predators but also to accidents and natural disasters such as grass fires. It most cases it is almost impossible to determine the fate of cubs that vanish; they simply disappear.

The only well-documented cause of tiger deaths seems to be encounters with porcupines, and until we came to Chitwan I always felt the historical accounts were slightly exaggerated. It seemed so unlikely that a large, efficient predator like the tiger would even bother to tangle with such small, prickly prey. However, among the villagers porcupines have a reputation for being exceedingly good to eat, some say second only to wild boar. When I first saw a porcupine shuffling about in the forest, it was much larger that I had expected, about forty pounds, the same weight as a barking deer. It moved relatively slowly, and to a young, hungry tiger who had never encountered such a creature before, it might seem like an easy meal. But there are few other animals that can cause such a slow, painful death.

Tigers have been shot or found dead with porcupine quills embedded in their chest, paws, mouth, neck and throat. In his book *Man-eaters of Kumaon*, Jim Corbett wrote: "I have extracted possibly a couple of hundred porcupine quills from the man-eaters I have shot. Many of these quills have been over nine inches long and as thick as pencils. The majority were embedded in hard muscles, a few were wedged firmly between bones and all were broken off short under the skin."

Porcupine quills have barbed ends, and once they penetrate the skin they are almost impossible to remove. The quills never dissolve, no matter how long they remain embedded, but work themselves deeper and deeper into the flesh.

Any further doubts I had about the lethal effect of porcupine quills were dispelled by a story Chuck told us. In the middle of the night, a male tiger cub had walked into the kitchen of the Khoria Mohan guardpost near Tiger Tops. He was the offspring of a tigress called Lakshmi, and Chuck had named him Bahadur and had kept tabs on him and his three siblings since they were a few months old. When the guards discovered Bahadur he was almost dead, barely able to raise his head. Incapacitated by a porcupine quill that had worked its way up into his shoulder, he had been unable to hunt. Starving and emaciated, he weighed less than half his proper weight. There was nothing anyone could do to save him, and he died a few minutes after Chuck arrived at the scene.

The other cause of mortality frequently mentioned in the old hunting literature is infanticide, male tigers killing cubs. Once again, there is truth to the stories, and there are a number of recent examples from Chitwan and from Kanha National Park in India. Most of the cubs involved were less than a year old, and many of them seem to have been killed while they and their mothers were feeding at a carcass. There is a much higher chance of encountering a male at a permanent bait site, because all the tigers in the area quickly learn the locations of these predictable food sources.

Why should male tigers kill cubs? There does not seem to be any wholly satisfactory explanation for every instance, but the accepted theory is derived from well-documented, long-term studies of lions and primates. A male lion has a fairly short tenure as the dominant male in a pride—two years seems to be the average—before he is ousted by a new group of males. The changeover of males is frequently accompanied by the disappearance of any small cubs in the pride; these cubs are often killed by the incoming males. With the death of their cubs, which were sired by the ousted group of male, lionesses quickly come into heat again and are mated by the new males. In view of their short tenure as breeding males, it seems that male lions are reluctant to wait for the cubs sired by the previous male to become independent and for their mothers to become sexually receptive again. If the existing cubs were allowed to live, the incoming males might have to wait as long as two years for the females to come into heat again. By then the males might have been ousted by a new group of males and have lost their only chance to breed.

Like lionesses, female tigers form the stable core of tiger society, and while there is not nearly as much information available about tigers, presumably the same conditions apply. In other words, a male can father cubs more quickly if he has killed the small cubs in his newly acquired territory. In Chitwan, three young male cubs from different litters were found dead after one male had taken over another's range; and in Kanha, H. R. Panwar also recorded several instances of males killing young cubs. All things considered, the chances of a female rearing a cub to independence are not very high, and a tigress is probably doing well if she averages one a year.

The biological success of male tigers is also measured by the number of their cubs that reach adulthood, but males do not play a direct role in raising their young. Instead, they reduce competition for food and minimize the chances of infanticide by keeping other males out of their areas. A male tiger maximizes the number of cubs he sires by maintaining a large territory, encompassing as many tigresses as possible. However, the area cannot be too large or he will not be able to hold onto it for long, and another male may take over and kill his offspring.

One incident in particular demonstrated how male ranges are won and lost. The Dakre Tiger had been the Sauraha Tiger's western

neighbor for almost three years. Their ranges did not overlap, and neither male intruded on the other's territory. However, during the monsoon of 1976 the Dakre Tiger was poisoned. While Chuck McDougal
and Dave Smith monitored the Sauraha Tiger from opposite ends of the
park, he gradually extended his range to include most of his former
neighbor's territory. Less than a month after the Dakre Tiger's death,
the Sauraha Tiger was found eight miles west of his previous boundary.
Five months later, his range had more than doubled in size; it was now
twenty-five miles long from east to west, and where formerly the Sauraha Tiger had four females with which he could mate, he now had
nine. Shortly afterward, another male entered the area and began
pushing eastward. The Sauraha Tiger retreated to a bait site near Tiger
Tops and stopped. Both males urine sprayed and scent marked intensively in the narrow area of overlap, but both continued to visit the
bait site.

The Sauraha Tiger now monopolized the breeding in the central
floodplain of the park. In the first year he mated with six tigresses, and
all produced cubs. However, he had to increase his travel rate to keep
this huge area under control; he visited and scent marked all parts of
his new, expanded range with the same frequency as he had monitored
his previous, smaller area, but he spent less time in any one place.

It is impossible to say how long the Sauraha Tiger could have
managed to hold on to this large piece of land because he died pre-
maturely, a few years later, in a freak accident. His death precipitated a
period of turmoil, and Chuck and Dave watched three or four younger
males trying to establish territories in the area that had once belonged
to one male. The struggle among the males also affected the tigresses.
Over the next two years, very few young were born, and several cubs
unaccountably disappeared. Obviously, unstable male ranges do not
provide a good environment in which females can raise cubs.

Our stay at Tiger Tops was all too brief, for on the following day
we had to return to camp to catch up on the activities of
the tigers near Sauraha. We would soon be leaving Nepal and had much
left to do. We and Chuck said goodbye with mutual regret, knowing it
would be some time before we saw each other again. He is an unusual
man, passionately committed to his long-term study of tigers and de-
termined that guests should be educated about wildlife as well as
pampered. In him, Chitwan tigers have a powerful advocate.

12   Last Days in Chitwan

SHORTLY AFTER WE RETURNED to Sauraha, the *zemindar* appeared on our doorstep. Although he wouldn't say so immediately, he had come to borrow one of our elephants and issue an invitation to a wedding. "*Namascar! Namascar!* Hello! Hello!" he trilled in his high, scratchy voice. Headman of the nearby village of Sauraha, local landlord, and revenue agent, the *zemindar* seemed to be in perpetual motion, always visiting people, checking on minor disputes, or simply en route from one place to another. An encounter with a sloth bear had left him with a badly scarred face and torso, but neither that nor his sixty-five years seemed to slow him down. He walked everywhere at top speed, his wiry body moving inside a baggy, wrinkled skin that was dusty at the knees and seemed too big for him.

I offered tea and he accepted, so we sat on wooden chairs arranged in a circle on the grass outside the house, making conversation. In Asia it is considered impolite to come to the point straightaway. After talk of crops, weather, and tourists, the conversation wandered slowly to the main point of the visit, the upcoming wedding of the *zemindar*'s grandson. It was to be a tremendous gathering, held in a neighboring village the next day. Preparations had been underway for months, and now the only thing lacking was an elephant for the procession. As Lord Ganesh, the Elephant God brings success and good luck to all ceremonies, and the *zemindar* was such a delightful old rogue, it would have been unthinkable to refuse him.

All the next day, processions of wailing wooden flutes, horns, and pounding drums accompanied guests and relatives on the long walk to the village of Jaimangala. To get to the wedding, guests and orchestras had to cross the Rapti River and walk two or three miles through the park. The dugout canoe was busy, ferrying twenty people at a time along with their bundles of bedding, bicycles, and baskets of chickens.

Impatient with waiting for the boat, some guests chose to wade at the waist-deep bullock-cart crossing. Squealing crowds of girls dressed in their best, laughing musicians, and glistening wet bullocks emerged on the other side to set off through the tall grass for the party.

We left for the wedding just before dusk, driving east to a more reliable river crossing. When we reached the ford, the water looked shallow, but halfway across, the engine spluttered and died, refusing to start again. We pushed the Jeep to the opposite bank and tinkered with it for some time under the interested gaze of a gathering crowd of on-lookers. Many of them were amateur mechanics or knew someone who once had had a car, so much friendly advice and moral support were offered. After half an hour, it became obvious that the engine could not be coaxed back to life by our mediocre skills or the combined will of the crowd, so we decided to proceed on foot like everybody else.

The zemindar *of Sauraha.*

We walked through the warm, scented twilight toward Jaimangala. Around us, small children hurried herds of livestock across the dusty plain toward stalls in the villages. The navy-blue sky was punctuated by millions of clear stars, and the smell of wood smoke mingled with the scent of spices. Soft, yellow light flickered through the walls and windows of the mud houses, and people called out greetings as we passed.

Although we had been invited to the wedding, there had been no time or address specified. We knew it was today, but our only directional cue was the distant sound of various orchestras converging on the site of the festivities. Trusting our ears, we wound along dusty paths and tracks that strung little clumps of houses together. Dogs snuffled in ditches searching for scraps, and every now and then a nightjar burst up from the rutted road in front of us. The sound of music and laughter grew closer.

Eventually we stumbled over a collection of quietly munching bullocks tethered by small piles of hay in the middle of the road. Near the bullocks was a jumbled arrangement of carts with red, tentlike awnings stretched over and around them. Women's muffled voices came from within. As we stepped around the bullocks in the dark, I asked Prem what the traffic jam was all about. "Brides," he whispered. "Brides are waiting here to be collected by the wedding party." I had expected only one bride, but it seemed that others were taking advantage of the occasion and getting married too.

The sound of a Nepali drum mingled with the abruptly rising and falling notes of horns and trumpets as we walked into the gathering place. It was an earthen courtyard hugged by neat mud-and-thatch houses and packed with people. Dozens of pressure lanterns strung from trees and poles cast an unreal, hard white light over the scene, and several different orchestras played independently and deafeningly in the confined space.

We stood uncertainly at the edge of the crowd, but the *zemindar* soon spotted us and darted over to greet us. He guided us toward an arrangement of wooden beds and handed round plates of fried goat-intestine *hors d'oeuvres* and glasses of the clear local liquor called *rakshi*. When the party was well underway, the scattered orchestras merged on some invisible signal and left the courtyard to collect the brides. They returned quickly with the festively covered wagons, and everyone crowded to the house where the marriages were to take place. We were introduced to the main groom, grandson of the *zemindar*. Only a portion of his face was visible under a white, shroudlike wrap, and he looked unhappy and very young. Prem said he was probably about fourteen, as the Tharu people tend to marry early. The bride was tiny and simi-larly invisible under a gorgeous red sari and embroidered veil that glit-tered and sparkled in the hissing lantern light. Enthusiastic onlookers pushed and crowded the couple, watching and participating in the tradi-tional exchange of gifts that included a broom, brass vessels, and rice.

After the marriage rites, there was a ceremonial meal. Ushered through a low doorway, we found ourselves in a large, airy room. In accordance with custom, we removed our shoes as we entered the house, good manners in Nepal where everyone sits on the floor. The room was quite bare by Western standards. A ten-foot-long, waist-high carved box held the family's rice supply. Other possessions were strung from the rafters—farm implements, sacks of grain or seed, and several woven baskets, each with a live hen settled snugly inside. Looking like a row of designer tea cosies, the fat, comfortable hens clucked softly at the intrusion and set their baskets swinging as they resettled them-selves.

Three shy Tharu girls offered bowls of fragrant goat curry accom-panied by plates of popped wheat. One of the *zemindar*'s male relatives stood by to refill our glasses. The fiery curry fueled our thirst, and our *rakshi* was replenished regularly until everything blurred. After the meal, we looked in briefly on the celebrations in the courtyard. The or-chestras were still enthusiastic but more disorganized, and the crowd was breaking up into smaller groups that clustered around several dif-ferent dancers, each of whom was pantomiming a different story. The party would go on into the morning or until everyone fell asleep.

Rather than walk the seven miles back through the villages to our inoperable Jeep, we decided to take the shorter route home, following the river along the inside edge of the park. Prem led the way with a flaming torch made from grass canes dipped in kerosene. His jaunty figure cast a huge, swaying shadow on the trees. The rest of us, with only one dim flashlight, followed trustingly. Our slightly inebriated state made us shy at shadows and sticks. The mashing, crunching sound of a rhino sent everyone into a panic, and for a while we walked bunched close together, treading on each other like a herd of nervous deer. Fortunately there was a little moonlight, and the well-trodden path was easy to follow. We half ran through the darkness, pursued by wild cries of birds and unidentifiable splashing noises.

Finally we stood at the river, where we had watched the laughing girls and bullock carts cross earlier in the day. The dugout canoe was nowhere in sight, so we whistled and called, bellowing "Dunga ho! Is the boat there?" but to no avail. The boatman was either drunk or at the party. There was no choice but to wade, clinging to each other in the waist-deep, swirling river. Reflections of bright stars whirled about us in the water as we struggled for footing on the shifting, sandy bottom. The current tugged at our clothes and tired us, making the hundred-yard crossing seem like a mile. Back at our house, we left our dripping clothes and shoes in a pile on the porch and crawled exhausted into bed.

The wedding had been another small glimpse into the lives of the people around us. At the start of the project, our major concern had been for the future of the tiger. We had not expected to feel much empathy for the people responsible for destroying the tigers' habitat. However, the people of Nepal welcomed us into their homes and their lives. From government officials and hotel owners in Kathmandu to villagers in Chitwan, people offered us hospitality and friendship. They also taught us a more realistic view of the problems of conserving wildlife in a less-developed country. They showed us that learning about the tigers' biology is only a tiny part of what is required to save the species. In Asia, the lives of people and wildlife are tightly interwoven. There is no longer enough room for it to be otherwise.

During the next several days, the wind changed direction and began to blow from the south, bringing hot, dry air from the heartland of India. Small, flat-bottomed clouds sailed quickly across the sky, building into thunderheads that spawned storms of awesome ferocity. Every few days, dark lines of wind and dust rolled in, turning the air ocher with stinging, blowing sand. It was difficult to walk or see and dangerous to be caught out in the whirling maelstrom of leaves, sticks, and dust.

Shrieking mobs of parakeets dived for cover into trees, and the tall grass twisted and writhed in the wind. On the heels of the wind and dust, the rain arrived as a wall of heavy, stinging drops, bombarding everything. Marble-sized hailstones mixed with the rain in a deafening roar as thunder and lightning boomed. These storms vanished as quickly as they came; suddenly there was no wind and the earth steamed in brilliantly clear sunlight. The heat was like a moist, suffocating blanket. Precursors of the monsoon, these storms reminded us that our time in Chitwan was drawing to a close.

There were important last-minute tasks to complete. Mel wanted to collect some more wet-season data on tiger movements so he could document the effects of flooding on tigers and their prey. We also needed to make one last attempt to locate the Roaring Tigress's brother, Tiger 104; he had disappeared about six months earlier, and we had not found him anywhere in the park. A Nepali friend who owned a farm near Kosi Tappu Reserve, about one hundred and forty miles east of Chitwan, had heard rumors of a tiger with a strap around its neck, so we decided to investigate. We listened over a wide area around the Kosi Reserve but did not pick up any radio signals, not too surprising as the batteries in the collar had probably given out. However, after talking with villagers in several different places, we became convinced that Tiger 104 had indeed managed to make it as far as the forest near Kosi Tappu. Several hunters and woodcutters had actually seen the tiger; one man who was hunting pigs had watched from some nearby bushes as the tiger drank from a small pool or water. He described it as having a bell around its neck. Another hunter from a village twenty miles away said he had seen a tiger with a white strap around its neck. The color was the most convincing piece of evidence we had heard, for before attaching the collars we always wrapped them in black electrical tape to protect them from the sun and make them less conspicuous. After a year or so the tape would fray and wear off, leaving the white plastic of the basic collar material exposed. We never actually saw the tiger with the strap around its neck, so we had no proof that it was Tiger 104. However, similar reports had come from hunters in widely separated villages, and since they were unlikely to have ever met, let alone collaborated on such an unlikely story, we came away feeling that they had seen the Roaring Tigress's brother.

Back in Chitwan, we started work earlier and earlier in the morning to avoid the worst of the heat, then spent the middle of the day immobile and drenched in sweat or wallowing in the river like rhinos. The tigers were obviously suffering from the heat too, as their daytime rest sites were almost always in or near the water. It rained more and more frequently and the rivers rose rapidly, boiling brown and frothy between the crumbling banks. One evening we counted sixty trees floating past in an hour and thought grimly of the erosion occurring in the hills.

Whenever the rain stopped for a few days the river receded, and we were sometimes able to cross into the park. Our last few trips on elephant back were unusually memorable, and we saw animals we had never seen before. On one occasion, a twelve-foot king cobra basked in the sun beside the road. Another day we saw the long, brown, fox-like shapes of two yellow-throated martens gazing down at us from the green gloom of the tree canopy.

When it was too dangerous to cross the river, we worked around the camp, taking last-minute photographs, sorting through equipment and data files, and packing deer jaws, tiger feces, and tracking gear. It was depressing to see the house in disarray, and to get away from the boxes and suitcases we went for long walks by the river, savoring our last moments in Chitwan.

Finally, it was time to leave. The Royal Nepal Airline flights from Bharatpur to Kathmandu were already being delayed for days because of the weather; if we waited any longer the rivers between Sauraha and the main road would be impassable. Goodbyes were difficult and we rushed to get them over with, but the *shikaris* and elephant men would not allow us leave quickly. They readied the elephants and gathered round to wish us well, moving me to tears with their farewell speeches. In a characteristically obstinate gesture, the Green Latrine refused to start, so we had to travel the five miles through the villages to Tardi Bazaar on elephant back. There we hitched a ride on a truck going to Bharatpur and the airport.

Although many more aspects of tiger social behavior remained to be investigated, we felt as if we had made a start. It would have been wonderful to stay on and continue the work, but Mel's contract was up and he was expected to return and write up the research results. The information would do no one, least of all the tigers, any good if it remained in our notebooks.

We had found that the excellent conditions in Chitwan, with its plentiful prey, cover, and water, supported the highest tiger density recorded anywhere in the world. Under these optimum conditions, females were able to meet their energy requirements in relatively small areas. Their social system of small, nonoverlapping ranges might be specific to these environmental conditions, but at least we had described one end of the continuum. Similarly, the adult males occupied exclusive areas, but their home ranges were several times larger than those of females. However, the spatial pattern of exclusive male and female ranges essentially sets limits on the number of tigers that can live within a given area, and it was obvious that beyond a certain level, one could not continue to pack more and more tigers into a park.

It was also evident that those tigresses living on the floodplain in Chitwan served as a breeding nucleus for the park. At any given time during the study, most of these tigresses were either pregnant or accompanied by two or three dependent cubs, and these females produced new litters about every two and a half years. Although the floodplain vegetation made up a comparatively small proportion (less than thirty percent) of the total area of the park, it was obviously the most important in terms of tiger reproduction. Tigresses living in sal forest reared fewer cubs, and they had ranges two or three times larger than those of tigresses living on the floodplain. This fact clearly illustrated that the overall size of a park or protected area was not necessarily the most important criterion.

While the floodplain habitats are critical for reproduction, we also learned that the value of sal forest should not be discounted, for it can serve as temporary habitat for young adults, especially males waiting for openings to appear in the core area. Older tigers, displaced from home ranges richer in prey, live out their lives in sal forest. Finally, we saw that sal forest can be a buffer, not just between resident and transient tigers, but between tigers and people and their livestock. As parks and reserves become completely surrounded by villages and increasingly isolated from one another, it will be more and more important to maintain areas of less-perfect habitat as places for dispersers and elderly tigers to live. Where buffer zones do not exist, these tigers will increasingly come into conflict with people and their livestock.

As tiger populations become isolated, there have been increased concerns over the deleterious effects of inbreeding, which include reduced female fertility and increased cub mortality. It has frequently been suggested that the inbreeding problem could be solved by capturing a male tiger in one reserve and transfering it into another, in order to introduce new genes into small populations that cannot mix through natural means, such as the migrations of tigers. However, our observations in Chitwan indicate that any future introductions or removals of breeding males as a means of trying to increase genetic variability are likely to have undesirable consequences, because they disrupt the social system. When there was a high turnover of males in Chitwan, matings were either unsuccessful or males killed cubs; few young were seen during these periods of flux. In addition, we observed vacant ranges being taken over so quickly that the timing of introductions would be very difficult, especially if several males native to the area were already waiting in the wings for a given home range to become vacant.

If Tiger 104 did manage to leave Chitwan, he got out just in time. The growth of local populations and the conversion of increasing amounts of forest and grassland into agricultural areas have rapidly isolated the park and its surrounding forest from any other tiger populations. After his study of tiger dispersal, Dave Smith concluded that "the Chitwan tigers constitute an isolated population . . ." and that there are "no practical means of establishing or maintaining corridors for tiger movement between the Chitwan population and those in the nearest reserves."

The Chitwan tiger population, however, is in good shape compared with tigers in many other reserves. At four hundred and sixteen square miles, Chitwan is the second-largest tiger reserve in the Indian subcontinent; there are an estimated one hundred and fifty to two hundred tigers in the park and surrounding forests, more than in most of the reserves in Asia. Unless disease sweeps through the population or there are dramatic changes in the vegetation with consequent effects on the prey and ultimately on the tiger, their long-term survival seems ensured.

Nepal's enormous increase in tourism has not been restricted to Kathmandu. In 1974, a total of eight hundred and thirty-six tourists visited Chitwan. Most stayed at Tiger Tops, and only a handful came to the almost-inaccessible village of Sauraha. We were so delighted to see visitors that we invited them in for a meal and took them out with us on the elephants to radio track tigers. Since then, a variety of small hotels and tea shops have been built in Sauraha, and in 1981 more than eight thousand tourists visited Chitwan. Many of the hotels offer two-day river-rafting trips from Kathmandu to Chitwan as part of a week-long adventure package, and a new road through the Mahabharats from Kathmandu to the *terai* means that the road trip to Chitwan now takes only about five hours.

This tenfold increase in the number of tourists has had a considerable impact on the area around Sauraha, where most of the new tourists have come. Pressure on the vegetation has been particularly noticeable in areas within easy reach of the hotels, and Itarni Island has undergone a dramatic change in the past ten years. In 1974, the vegetation was so dense and tangled that there were only two major trails wide enough for an elephant to travel on. The one-square-mile island contained a large population of deer, rhino, and wild boar, enough prey to support the Roaring Tigress when she reached maturity and moved out of Number One's range. Today the vegetation is battered and broken, weed species proliferate, and it is possible to go anywhere on an elephant. Each hotel sends several elephant loads of tourists onto the island every day in search of wildlife, and over-enthusiastic drivers smash down bushes and small trees to give their passengers a better view. The once-pristine riverine forest has degenerated so dramatically that it can no longer support enough prey to sustain even a single tiger.

Human activities have influenced the tigers in other, less obvious ways as well. After we followed the Sauraha Tiger around for several months, it became obvious that tigers make extensive use of roads and trails. Dave Smith was convinced that the roads in Chitwan were a major factor in the Sauraha Tiger's ability to maintain such a large range after he took over part of the Dakre Tiger's area. Without the road, it would have taken the Sauraha Tiger longer to make the east-west trip, and he probably would not have been able to get around frequently enough to maintain exclusive rights to the area. Perhaps an extensive network of roads can contribute to reducing the number of breeding males in an area.

Neighbors can also influence the size of a tiger's territory. Chitwan National Park is long and narrow, bordered on the north by the Rapti River and agricultural land. Tigers whose home ranges butted up against this barrier of people and crops did not have to worry about encroachment from a neighboring tiger in that area and could spend more time scent marking in other parts of their own home ranges. We felt sure this factor allowed males to maintain larger territories and monopolize more females than they would have been able to do under different circumstances. Theoretically, a park of the same size but roughly circular in shape could contain more tigers.

Nepal is facing a serious environmental crisis. The magnitude of the problems are such that they affect much of the subcontinent, all the way to India and Bangladesh. The crisis is largely one of people and land. Only fourteen percent of Nepal's land area is arable, compared with fifty percent of India's land. Because such a high proportion of the country is vertical, the soil is easily washed away; deforestation is causing Nepal to lose a staggering amount of its irreplaceable topsoil every year. The country can ill afford this loss, for each two and a half acres of land support nearly nine people, one of the highest ratios in Southeast Asia.

Despite these pressures, Nepal is passionately committed to saving the tiger. His Majesty King Birendra himself has indicated clearly that wildlife conservation is a high priority, and there is a cadre of well-educated scientists in prominent positions within both the Wildlife and Forest Departments who can carry out this mandate. Despite the almost overwhelming problems of preserving potentially prime agricultural areas for wildlife in the midst of a land crisis, the tiger and its ecosystem are regarded as a national heritage and have become a symbol of what the country stands to lose.

Our flight to Delhi was scheduled to leave Kathmandu at seven in the evening. As always, the appointed time was only a guideline and the plane was late, but it didn't really matter. As the jet rumbled through the black sky, we settled back in our seats and thought about the many times we had sat by the fire in Chitwan, listening to the

Delhi flight pass overhead. Our friends would be sitting there tonight. The tigers we had come to know as individuals would be stalking through the wet forests, marking their ranges, making kills, and raising cubs. Number One, the Roaring Tigress, the Sauraha Tiger—we sadly accepted that we would never see these tigers again. But we knew that they, and then their descendants, would continue to stalk the grasslands and forests of Chitwan: Nepal will not let the tiger slip away.

Acknowledgments

This work would not have been possible without the help of several organizations and numerous individuals to whom we wish to express our sincere thanks.

Generous financial support for the project was provided throughout its entirety by the Smithsonian Institution and the World Wildlife Fund (U. S. Appeals). We would like to acknowledge the personal interest and constant support of S. Dillon Ripley, former Secretary of the Smithsonian Institution; David Challinor, Assistant Secretary for Science, Smithsonian Institution; and Ross Simons, Project Administrator, Smithsonian Institution. Without their contributions the work could not have been completed.

The investigation of tigers, leopards, and their prey in Royal Chitwan National Park has been a cooperative effort between the Smithsonian Institution and the National Parks and Wildlife Conservation Department, His Majesty's Government of Nepal. The enthusiasm and support of government officials during the study are greatly appreciated, and many people in the Ministry of Forests were very helpful and cooperative in all phases of the project. A few of the individuals who gave so generously of their time and skills include A. R. Rajbhandari, T. B. Rayamajhi, and Emerald J. B. Rana. We are also grateful to B. N. Upreti, Chief, National Parks and Wildlife Conservation Department, His Majesty's Government of Nepal; and former Chiefs B. B. Shah and P. B. S. Pradhan. We would also like to thank former park wardens Tirtha Maskey and J. K. Tamrakar for their help.

In particular, we wish to thank Kirti Man Tamang, coprincipal investigator on the project, and his wife Pat; and B. L. Tharu and Bodai Tharu. All other *shikaris* and elephant men and their families at the camp contributed to making the study a truly memorable experience: D. L. Tharu, Vishnu Tamang, Man Bahadur, Man Sing, Haarka Man, Kancha Lama, Hit Bahadur, Bul Bahadur, Bir Bahadur, Dal Bahadur, Bikram,

Phirta, Gyan Bahadur, Hernan, Jai Bahadur, Colera, "Kasi Babu," Birja Lal, Ganesh Bahadur, Buddi Ram, Ram Bahadur, and Lauray all have our thanks. Pralad Yonzon and Sagar Timilsina, project assistants, did a remarkable job, especially during the period of Kirti's recovery after he was mauled by a tigress. We would especially like to thank Prem B. Rai, *subedar* of *shikaris*, for allowing us to witness and partake in his understanding of tracks and signs. His knowledge made a significant contribution to the project.

Through numerous discussions with Dave Smith, Chuck McDougal, John Seidensticker, and Hemanta Mishra, our understanding of tigers in Chitwan, and of Chitwan itself, has been greatly enhanced. All have contributed in many other ways as well by helping to capture, tag, and radio track tigers and by keeping us up to date on the whereabouts and activities of known and new tigers in the park. We sincerely appreciate their hospitality, friendship, advice, help, and cooperation.

Hemanta and Sushma Mishra, Dave Smith and Francie Cuthbert, and Chuck and Margie McDougal generously invited us to stay with them and made us feel at home on our return trips to Nepal. All willingly shared their time and allowed us to be part of their families on many occasions; we could not have made better friends.

We would also like to thank Clara Daniels for her help while we were writing this book. Bob Pratt painted the relief map of Nepal, and we are grateful for his talented contribution.

Finally, we deeply appreciate the encouragement, wisdom, and endless patience of Susan Abrams and Judith Hayter. Without their help this book would never have been started or completed.

Glossary of Nepali Terms

Bagh	Tiger
Bhit	White cloth used in tiger capture operation
Chowki	Guardpost
Cul	Elephant command, meaning "Put out foot"
Dek	Elephant command, meaning "Look"
Dun	Valley in the lower Himalayan foothills
Dunga	Dugout canoe
Hathi	Elephant
Hatizar	Elephant camp
Machan	Shooting or observation platform
Mahut	Elephant caretaker
Namascar	Greetings
Nullah	Ravine or valley
Pachhuwa	Elephant caretaker
Phanit	Elephant driver
Rakshi	Home-brewed liquor
Roh	Elephant command, meaning "Stand still"
Shikari	Tracker or hunting guide
Subedar	Chief or headman
Tal	Oxbow lake
Terai	Lowland region
Tharu	Oldest known inhabitants of the terai region
Zemindar	Village headman, local landlord

The Large Mammals of Chitwan

Common name	Scientific name
Rhesus monkey	*Macaca mulatta*
Common langur	*Presbytis entellus*
Indian hare	*Lepus nigricollis*
Indian porcupine	*Hystrix indica*
Jackal	*Canis aureus*
Indian wild dog	*Cuon alpinus*
Indian fox	*Vulpes bengalensis*
Sloth bear	*Melursus ursinus*
Smooth Indian otter	*Lutra perspicillata*
Spotted linsang	*Prionodon pardicolor*
Common mongoose	*Herpestes edwardsi*
Crab-eating mongoose	*Herpestes urva*
Tody cat	*Paradoxurus hermaphroditus*
Large Indian civet	*Viverra zibetha*
Small Indian civet	*Viverricula indica*
Yellow-throated marten	*Martes flavigula*
Binturong	*Arctictis binturong*
Ratel	*Mellivora carpensis*
Jungle cat	*Felis chaus*
Fishing cat	*Felis viverrina*
Leopard	*Panthera pardus*
Tiger	*Panthera tigris*
Domesticated elephant	*Elephas maximus*

179

Gaur	Bos gaurus
Wild Pig	Sus scrofa
Barking deer	Muntiacus muntjak
Chital or spotted deer	Axis axis
Hog deer	Axis porcinus
Sambar	Cervus unicolor
Serow	Capricornis sumatraensis
Four-horned antelope	Tetraceros quadricornis
One-horned rhinoceros	Rhinoceros unicornis

Species formerly found in Chitwan

Swamp deer or barasingha	Cervus duvauceli
Wild water buffalo	Bubalus bubalis
Wild elephant	Elephas maximus

References

Anderson, M. M. 1977. *The Festivals of Nepal.* Calcutta: Rupa and Co.

Bhat, D. D. 1970 *Natural History and Economic Botany of Nepal.* Calcutta: Orient Longman Ltd.

Bragin, A. P. 1986. Territorial behavior and possible regulatory mechanisms of population density in the Amur tiger (*Panthera tigris altaica*). *Zoologicheskii Zhurhal* 65:272–282.

Corbett, J. 1944. *Man-eaters of Kumaon.* London: Penguin Books Ltd.

Desai, J. H. 1973. Observations on the reproductive biology and early postnatal development of the panther *Panthera pardus* L. in captivity. *Journal of the Bombay Natural History Society* 72:293–304.

Dunbar Brander, A. A. 1923. *Wild Animals in Central India.* London: Edward Arnold and Co.

Eaton, R. L. 1977. Reproductive biology of the leopard. *Der Zoologische Garten* (NF) 47:329–351.

Fleming, R. L., Sr., R. L. Fleming, Jr., and L. S. Bandgel. 1976. *Birds of Nepal.* Bombay: Vakil and Sons Ltd.

Forsyth, J. 1871. *The Highlands of Central India.* London: Chapman and Hall.

Gee, E. P. 1964. *The Wild Life of India.* London: William Collins.

Gurung, K. K. 1983. *Heart of the Jungle.* London: André Deutsch Ltd.

Hooker, J. D. 1855. *Himalayan Journals. Notes of a Naturalist in Bengal, the Sikkim, and Nepal Himalayas.* London: John Murray.

International Union for Conservation of Nature and Natural Resources, Cat Specialist Group. 1985. Cat News No. 3., August. Gland, Switzerland: International Union for Conservation of Nature and Natural Resources.

Jackson, P. 1985. Man-eaters. *International Wildlife* 15(6):4–11.

Kleiman, D. G. 1974. The estrous cycle of the tiger (*Panthera tigris*). In *The World's Cats*, vol. 2, edited by R. L. Eaton. Winston, Oregon: World Wildlife Safari.

Kotwal, P. C. 1984. Incidences of intraspecific fights and cannibalism among tigers in Kanha National Park, India. Paper presented at International Union for Conservation of Nature and Natural Resources Cat Specialist Group Workshop, Kanha National Park, India.

Laurie, W. A. 1978. The Ecology and Behaviour of the Greater One-horned Rhinoceros. Doctoral dissertation, University of Cambridge, England.

McDougal, C. 1977. *The Face of the Tiger*. London: Rivington Books.

McDougal, C. 1981. Some observations on tiger behaviour in the context of baiting. *Journal of the Bombay Natural History Society* 77 : 476–485.

Milton, J. P., and G. A. Binney. 1980. *Ecological Planning in the Nepalese Terai. A Report on Resolving Resource Conflicts between Wildlife Conservation and Agricultural Land Use in Padampur Panchayat*. Washington, D. C.: Threshold, International Center for Environmental Renewal.

Mishra, H. R. 1982. Balancing human needs and conservation in Nepal's Royal Chitwan Park. *Ambio* 11 : 246–252.

Mishra, H. R. 1982. The Ecology and Behaviour of Chital (*Axis axis*) in the Royal Chitwan National Park, Nepal. (With Comparative Studies of Hog Deer [*Axis porcinus*], Sambar [*Cervus unicolor*], and Barking Deer [*Muntiacus muntjak*]). Doctoral dissertation, University of Edinburgh, Scotland.

Molnar, P., and P. Tapponnier. 1977. The collision between India and Eurasia. *Scientific American* 236 : 30–42.

Packer, C. 1986. The ecology of sociality in felids. In *Ecological Aspects of Social Evolution*, edited by D. I. Rubenstein and R. W. Wrangham. Princeton, N.J.: Princeton University Press.

Panwar, H. R. 1979. Population dynamics and land tenures of tigers in Kanha National Park, India. Paper presented at International Symposium on Tiger, New Delhi, India.

Perry, R. 1965. *The World of the Tiger*. London: Atheneum.

Prater, S. H. 1971. *The Book of Indian Animals*. Bombay: Bombay Natural History Society.

Rogers. L. L. 1977. Movements and Spatial Relationships of Black Bears in Northeastern Minnesota. Doctoral dissertation, University of Minnesota, Minneapolis.

Schaller, G. B. 1967. *The Deer and the Tiger: A Study of Wildlife in India*. Chicago: University of Chicago Press.

Seidensticker, J. 1976. On the Ecological Separation between Tigers and Leopards. *Biotropica* 8 : 225–234.

Seidensticker, J. 1977. Notes on Early Maternal Behavior of the Leopard. *Mammalia* 41 : 111–113.

Seidensticker, J., M. E. Sunquist, and C. McDougal. 1983. Leopards living at the edge of Royal Chitwan National Park, Nepal. Paper presented at Bombay Natural History Society Centenary Symposium on Conservation in Developing Countries, Bombay, India.

Seifert, S. 1978. Untersuchungen zur Fortpflanzungsbiologie der im Zoologischen Garten Leipzig gehaltenen Grosskatzen (*Panthera*, Oken, 1816) unter besonderer Berücksichtngung des Löwen *Panthera leo* (Linné 1758). Berlin: VEB Verlag Volk und Gesundheit.

Smith, J. L. D. 1984. Dispersal, Communication, and Conservation Strategies for the Tiger (*Panthera tigris*) in Royal Chitwan National Park, Nepal. Doctoral dissertation, University of Minnesota, St. Paul.

Smith, J. L. D., C. McDougal, and M. E. Sunquist. 1987. Female land tenure system in tigers. In *Tigers of the World: The Biology, Management, and Biopolitics of Conservation of an Endangered Species*, edited by R. L. Tilson and U. S. Seal. Park Ridge, N. J., Noyes Publications.

Smythies, E. A. 1942. *Big Game Shooting in Nepal*. Calcutta: Thacker, Spink and Co.

Soulé, M. E., editor. 1986. *Conservation Biology: The Science of Scarcity and Diversity*. Sunderland, Mass.: Sinauer Associates, Inc., Publishers.

Stainton, J. D. A. 1972. *Forests of Nepal*. London: John Murray.

Sunquist, F. C. 1984. Cut and burn in a Nepal park: all in the plan. *Smithsonian* (March): 164–169.

Sunquist, M. E. 1981. The Social Organization of Tigers (*Panthera tigris*) in Royal Chitawan National Park, Nepal. *Smithsonian Contributions to Zoology* No. 336. Washington, D. C.: Smithsonian Institution Press.

Sunquist, M. E. 1983. Dispersal of three radiotagged leopards. *Journal of Mammalogy* 64: 337–341.

Sunquist, M. E., and H. R. Mishra. 1983. Habitat utilization and movement patterns of tigers and their prey: implications for management and reserve design. Paper presented at Bombay Natural History Society Centenary Symposium on Conservation in Developing Countries, Bombay, India.

Thapar, V. 1986. *Tiger: Portrait of a Predator*. London: William Collins.

Wemmer, C., R. Simons, and H. R. Mishra. 1983. Case history of a cooperative international conservation program: the Smithsonian Nepal Tiger Ecology Project. Paper presented at Bombay Natural History Society Centenary Symposium on Conservation in Developing Countries, Bombay, India.

Zajonc, R. B. 1971. Attraction, affiliation and attachment. In *Man and Beast: Comparative Social Behavior*, edited by J. F. Eisenberg and W. S. Dillon. Washington, D. C.: Smithsonian Institution Press.

Index

185